Growing
The
Fruit
Of
The
Spirit

Deborah Lynne

Sand & Sea Publishing

COPYRIGHT

Growing the Fruit of The Spirit is a book inspired by God to Deborah Lynne, © ***October 2023.***

The thoughts and understandings are Deborah Lynne's while reading God's Word from YouVersion's The Holy Bible ...using YouVersion's Translations of GNT (Good News Translation), NLT (New Living Translation), and/or NIV (New International Version).

All Scripture quotations are taken and noted from YouVersion's, NLT copyright 1996, 2004, 2007, 2015 by Tyndale House Foundation., NIV © 1973, 1978, 1984, 2011 by Biblical Inc and/or GNT (Good News Translation - Today's English Version Second Edition) 1992 American Bible Society.

Deborah Lynne encourages you to read all the contents and receive the messages in this writing encouraged by God to Deborah through His Word, feed on it, believe His Word for yourself, and then share Him with your family, friends, and neighbors.

Cover design by E Y Grant © ***October 2023*** and published by Sand & Sea Publishing. Cover art purchased from Shutterstock, image ID#1064235809.

Let God's light shine through you!

Visit the author's website—www.author-deborahlynne.com[1]

---

1.   http://www.author-deborahlynne.com

Foreword

Deborah Lynne has a gift taking you into the scene and feeling the intensity, suspense and the peace of God's love in her writings. Looking for a quick, exciting read Deborah Lynne's your author. ... Ellen E., entrepreneur

Deborah's latest book is a testament to her deep faith and love of God. Filled with her belief that knowing God can bless us, she shares her own perspective on how to understand God's influence on our lives. She urges us to invite him into our hearts so that we can be all that we can be. ... E Y Grant, author, friend, and sister in Christ

The only thing almost as important to Deborah as her relationship with God, is using her gift of writing to help others develop their own relationship with Him. Reading Deborah's books will leave you not only knowing more about God, but desiring more OF God also. ... Pete M, Book narrator and Author

Deborah fearlessly explores life's big questions with strong beliefs and a compassionate heart. Get ready to be challenged, inspired, and touched by words that will help you to reflect and be changed. Deborah clearly is a willing vessel, allowing God to work through her to touch her readers. ... Molly Moore, Transformation Coach and Author

Having known Deborah Lynne for many years, I have witnessed firsthand the embodiment of the Fruit of the Spirit in her life. Her book, 'Growing the Fruit of The Spirit,' is a testament to her deep and authentic journey with God. It's a profound guide, rich in scriptural wisdom and practical insights, that invites readers to cultivate the same spiritual fruit in their own lives. Deborah's heartfelt and accessible writing makes this book an essential resource for anyone yearning to grow closer to God and reflect Christ's love and grace more fully in their daily walk. ... Jonathan Stock-still, Pastor

Preface

The Lord encouraged me to share with my readers about the Fruit of the Spirit, the gift He gives each of us who ask Him into our hearts as our Lord and Savior. And I encourage you, the reader, to fill your heart with the message He gave me to share with you.

He led me to write about the Fruit of the Spirit that He wants to grow in each of us — making us more and more like Him. I hope after reading my book you will have a better understanding and knowledge of the Fruit of the Spirit living in you, the believer, and how you can grow the Spirit living in you, helping you walk more in the Spirit and less in the flesh.

When we, as believers, asked Jesus into our heart to be our Savior, He gave us the gift of the Holy Spirit living in us—— and He wants us to grow in each part, each character trait, of the Fruit of the Spirit, so we can become more and more like Him.

I hope I share all that God gives me to share with you in an easy to understand way, and that I share His Word backing up what He is telling me to say.

His Word is final. It is the whole truth. If I misspeak or misinterpret something, forgive me. Use His Word to be the final say.

God bless you all who take the time to read this new book, ***Growing The Fruit of The Spirit***. God placed this message on my heart to share with everyone who takes time to read it.

I love Him and I live to be all He has called me to be.

Here is a prayer I pray over all of you who are reading my book.

Dear Heavenly Father, help each of us walk in the fruit of the Spirit...the Spirit You gave each of us who has accepted you as our Savior. Let all of your traits be reflected in all we do as You grow the fruit of the Spirit in us.

In Jesus' name I pray. Amen.

Thank You Lord!

Praise You Lord!

INTRODUCTION

In the book, ***Growing the Fruit of the Spirit***, I hope to share what the Fruit of the Spirit is, and what I believe God's Word means for the Holy Spirit to be for each of us who believe in Jesus as our Lord and Savior.

Originally, I thought my book would be called growing the fruits of the Spirit, but as I started reading and researching more and more on the fruit of the Spirit, I learned it is Fruit, not Fruits, of the Spirit ... the fruit of the Holy Spirit contains nine parts, or should I say nine traits.

One believer helped me to think of it like an orange, and how the orange is one whole fruit but made up of several sections, growing them together building that one luscious fruit...the juicy delectable orange. So that is how I think of the Holy Spirit—one spirit with nine glorious character traits...all that filled Jesus as He walked the earth.

The Holy Spirit in us is one Spirit with nine traits, given to us from Jesus. He told us when He goes, He will leave the Holy Spirit in all of us who believe in Jesus as their Savior. Each of these traits are living in Jesus, and now living in us!

He wants to help us grow each trait within us, making us more and more like Jesus every day. The more we grow in each trait, the stronger we will become in our faith in Him, resting and trusting Him to lead us and using us to grow the Kingdom of God.

As you grow the fruit of the Spirit within you, you will be filling your Spirit man with loads of love, joy, peace, patience, kindness, goodness, faithfulness, gentleness, and self-control making you more free and liberated and making you more and more Christ-like.

And you will share these wonderful Godly traits with others the more you grow in the Spirit.

Oh what a blessing you will be to all around you as you let the Holy Spirit lead you as each trait of the Holy Spirit grows within you, making your Spirit-filled reflection of Jesus strong in you, making you a major blessing to all around you. Others will want to have what you have, Jesus Christ as your LORD and Savior. Talk about growing the kingdom of God.

That is what you will be doing. Praise God.

I hope you enjoy my new book. God bless you!

DEDICATION

I dedicate *Growing the Fruit of The Spirit* to God. He has blessed me to write it and I am so thankful and grateful that He trusts me to do so.

Through all of my books, my fiction and my non-fiction, I am blessed to be able to share His love, His goodness, His mercy, His grace, and the fact that He will never leave us nor forsake us.

Praise God!!!

I dedicate this book to you, the reader, as well. Thank you for joining me in my love for the Lord by reading the books He encourages me to write.

As long as we keep connected to Him through the reading and the listening of His Word, He will stay connected to us. His Word tells us so.

God wants a personal relationship with each and every one of us.

And know He will help us grow in living the lives that He has called us to live...A life growing the Kingdom of God.

How does He grow us?

By growing the fruit of the Spirit within us.

I hope my book, *Growing the Fruit of The Spirit,* helps to lead and direct you to grow the fruit of the Spirit in you more and more, helping you to become more like Jesus Christ, our Lord and Savior...becoming more Christ-like in your everyday life.

What a fabulous way to share the Lord, by walking through your life reflecting Him!!!

SCRIPTURE

Galatians 5:16 (GNT) - *What I say is this: let the Spirit direct your lives, and you will not satisfy the desires of the human nature.*

Galatians 5:22-23 (GNT) - *But the Spirit produces love, joy, peace, patience, kindness, goodness, faithfulness, humility and self-control. There is no law against such things as these.*

GROWING THE FRUIT OF THE SPIRIT

Love, joy, peace, patience (forbearance), kindness, goodness, faithfulness, gentleness (humility), and self-control are the various characteristics that are contained in the fruit of the Spirit, the Holy Spirit. We were blessed by Jesus when we accepted Him as our Lord and Savior to be filled with the Holy Spirit.

When we became believers in Jesus Christ as our Lord and Savior, God infilled us with the Holy Spirit. He gifted us with the Holy Spirit. The Holy Spirit lives in us to give us added spiritual strength. He gives us added spiritual direction too, but we have to learn to listen to the Holy Spirit within us. We have to learn to rely on the Holy Spirit for the answers we are searching for. To do this we must grow the Holy Spirit within us by feeding ourselves with the Word—by filling the Holy Spirit with praises as we sing out and shout out our love for God. The Holy Spirit doesn't come in and just take over—we have to relinquish our fleshly, natural responses to the Holy Spirit's responses.

God gives us the freedom of choice—the choice between living by our flesh or letting the Holy Spirit in us lead. It is so easy to just let the flesh lead. In fact, that was how we were created, before the Holy Spirit came to live within us, we the believers of Jesus Christ as our Lord and Savior.

So we as believers in Jesus must learn to surrender ourselves totally to the Holy Spirit.

When we take time to read the Gospels of the Holy Bible we see all these wonderful characteristics coming out through Jesus as He lives and walks in His daily life.

And as a believer in Him, we want to become more and more like Him. So we want to grow the fruit of the Spirit in us.

The fruit of the Holy Spirit is the effect, or result, of living the Christian life in obedience. It is what *flows* in those believers who resist the "works of the flesh," and follow the Holy Spirit from within.

How do we do this?

When we walk or live in the natural, we are living in our own power, our own strength. So we get tired, worn down, discouraged. BUT when we live in the Holy Spirit, when we start depending on the Holy Spirit to lead us and direct us, He will take the burdens off of our shoulders.

The Holy Spirit will strengthen us to keep moving forward in our ministry—in our life.

The power of God is in you. God infilled you with the Holy Spirit. Use it to grow in your life and your calling by God. Grow your relationship with the Holy Spirit that is already inside you (a free gift from God) by getting deep into the Word, by praying and talking with the Lord, by being more like Jesus as you learn what Jesus would do in any situation you are put into—or any situation that comes into your life. Grow your relationship with the Holy Spirit by spending more time and thought on Jesus.

We as followers, try to grow the Christ-like character in us. As we do, it brings us closer to being the person we were designed to be—-living in the Spirit not in the flesh. Being a Christian means living by the Spirit. This should show in our daily lives. As the Holy Spirit dwells in our (Christian) hearts, the Holy Spirit should become visible in the "fruit" we bear. Living by faith is us being transformed by the Spirit in us...living according to God's will, trusting Him to lead us by the Spirit He placed in us. And as we do, we pour God's love out on others around us, drawing them toward Him, planting the seed in others around us and watering it till the seed is nurtured and they call Him into their lives. A seed planted and/or nurtured by us sharing Him.

Let the Holy Spirit be your constant companion leading you, comforting you and helping you through each and every day of your life. He is there—in you—wanting to be active and in control. Let go of self and relinquish control to the Holy Spirit in you.

Luke 4:14 - (NLT) - *Then Jesus returned to Galilee, filled with the Holy Spirit's power. Reports about him spread quickly through the whole region.*

The scripture above tells us the Holy Spirit living in Jesus was Jesus' power! Jesus is God in the flesh. And the Holy Spirit is God in the spirit. That is the Holy Trinity in one - God the father, the Son, and the Holy Spirit.

Praise God...He gave us the Holy Spirit so we too can have supernatural power to get through life here on earth! Thank You Jesus!

The Holy Spirit is the perfect guide for we believers in Jesus Christ to be led through the twists and turns in our lives today and every day. Rest on Him. Trust in Him.

Romans 8:14 - (NLT) - *For all who are led by the Spirit of God are children of God.*

The good news is we don't have to earn the Holy Spirit's help. He is there for us. He was given to us to help us through our lives as a gift from God. But we have to choose to take the Holy Spirit's help.

Acts 2:38 (GNT) - *Peter said to them, "Each one of you must turn away from your sins and be baptized in the name of Jesus Christ, so that your sins will be forgiven; and you will receive God's gift, the Holy Spirit.*

We have to let go of our our natural, fleshly responses to let the Holy Spirit lead us in responding as Jesus would.

Again, it's still our choice to live in the Spirit or live in the flesh...Choose wisely.

Galatians (GNT) 5:16-18 - *What I say is this: let the Spirit direct your lives, and you will not satisfy the desires of the human nature. For what our human nature wants is opposed to what the*

Spirit wants, and what the Spirit wants is opposed to what our human nature wants. These two are enemies, and this means that you cannot do what you want to do. If the Spirit leads you, then you are not subject to the Law.

So let the Spirit lead you in your life—NOT your flesh!

He has great plans for each and every one of us who choose Him to be our Savior. His Word tells us so.

The fruit of the Spirit manifests itself in a believer's life in two ways. Sometimes it just flows out, spontaneously. Someone does something for you or a friend and love just pops out. You can't help yourself because the Holy Spirit in you responded naturally in love...you the believer were letting the Holy Spirit be in charge, in control.

Wouldn't it be lovely if every day and every moment of our lives we spontaneously let the Holy Spirit react from within.

Sad to say, that doesn't always happen, even for the strongest believer. Sometimes we struggle.

What should we do when our flesh wants to respond?

We have to remind ourselves of what the Word tells us...keep no record of wrongs, forgive and move on...let the Lord handle any vengeance you think might be needed. You walk in love and let God handle the retaliation, if there is something needed to be paid back or repaid. Let God handle it...not you. Let the Holy Spirit lead you, not your flesh.

You have to intentionally force yourself to keep no record of wrongs; you have to refuse to point the finger. You have to work at it daily. You have to die to the flesh. And *because* you have the Holy Spirit living in you, *you can do it.* Yesterday was easy...maybe. But today was not so easy. But you have to remember, you can do all things through Christ who lives in you through the Holy Spirit. Keep your focus on God's Word and on how He wants you to react every day in every situation. Keep moving forward...one day at a time. Keep renewing your mind with His Word and keep living how the Holy Spirit leads you.

Jeremiah 29:11-13 (GNT) - *"I alone know the plans I have for you, plans to bring you prosperity and not disaster, plans to bring about the future you hope for. Then you will call to me. You will come and pray to me, and I will answer you. You will seek me, and you will find me because you will seek me with all your heart.*

He goes on to tell us the Spirit of God lives in us...the same Spirit that raised Jesus from the dead. And as God raised Christ Jesus from the dead, He will give life to us and our mortal bodies by the Holy Spirit living within us. Thank You God!

Romans 8:11 (GNT) - *If the Spirit of God, who raised Jesus from death, lives in you, then he who raised Christ from death will also give life to your mortal bodies by the presence of his Spirit in you.*

The character traits of Jesus; love, joy, peace, patience, kindness, goodness, faithfulness, gentleness, and self-control together all make up the fruit of the Holy Spirit living in you when you asked Jesus to come into your life.

When the fruit of the Spirit is revealed in us in the way we live our lives, it's a sign that we are being led by the Spirit of God, not by our flesh. So let His fruit be reflected in your actions. Let others see Jesus in you.

When we follow our own flesh instead of the Holy Spirit in us we tend to walk in sinful ways...ways not pleasing to God. When we walk in the flesh we are trying to satisfy our human desires.

We can't please both...flesh and Spirit.

We have to choose one—walk in the flesh or walk in the Spirit. As a believer, we must choose to let the Spirit in us lead us...not our flesh.

Galatians 5:16-18 (NIV) - *So I say, walk by the Spirit, and you will not gratify the desires of the flesh. For the flesh desires what is contrary to the Spirit, and the Spirit what is contrary to the flesh.*

They are in conflict with each other, so that you are not to do whatever you want. But if you are led by the Spirit, you are not under the law.

The two are in constant conflict with each other. So let the Holy Spirit lead you in your life...not your flesh!

Jesus sent the Holy Spirit to live in all who believes in Him as their Lord and Savior. We are never alone because He is always in us. He gives us power to conquer the sin that always tries to seep into our lives.

Keep praying, asking God to let the Holy Spirit in you take the lead...the lead in your thoughts, in your actions, and in your reactions. Ask the Holy Spirit to be in total control. Think Jesus first..and self last.

You know the Holy Spirit lives in you, but to give Him the lead is up to you.

The good news is when we choose to walk in the Spirit there is no limit on how much love, joy, peace, patience, kindness, goodness, faithfulness, gentleness, and self-control we can pour out on others. The more we walk in these traits pouring them out on others, the more we bless others and in turn, are blessed ourself. God loves for us to reflect Jesus in our lives.

A question sometimes asked is, "Are the Spiritual gifts God gives us the same as the Fruit of the Spirit?

No.

The gifts the Spirit gives us are inside of us, like the Holy Spirit is in each of us who believe Jesus Christ as Lord and Savior, and we are to use the gifts to help others become aware of Christ, like the Holy Spirit wants to lead us to walk in love, patience, joy, peace and so much more for others. The spiritual gifts He gives us are special abilities He gives us to help us grow the Kingdom of God.

In the Bible, these special abilities are called spiritual gifts. These are different from material or physical gifts. They are the abilities you need to get the job done that God wants you to do. Many people who are believers don't even know they've got them, much less what they are.

But you have them! We, His children, all do. And you can learn what they are as you grow in your relationship with the Lord.

While praying, you ask Him to reveal to you His plans for you. Ask Him to reveal to you the gifts He has given you to share with others to help them learn more about Him, so they too can join the Kingdom of God and have a personal relationship with the Lord.

You can't earn your spiritual gifts nor do you deserve them — that's why they are called gifts! They are an expression of God's grace to you and me, we who believe in Jesus Christ as our Lord and Savior.

We also can't choose which gift, or gifts, we have. Paul explains that God determines that, and the Holy Spirit distributes all these special gifts to the one God chose. He alone decides which gift or gifts each person should have. He tells us this in 1 Corinthians 12:11.

1 Corinthians 12:1-11 (GNT) - *Now, concerning what you wrote about the gifts from the Holy Spirit. I want you to know the truth about them, my friends. You know that while you were still heathen, you were led astray in many ways to the worship of lifeless idols. I want you to know that no one who is led by God's Spirit can say "A curse on Jesus!" And no one can confess "Jesus is Lord," without being guided by the Holy Spirit. There are different kinds of spiritual gifts, but the same Spirit gives them. There are different ways of serving, but the same Lord is served. There are different abilities to perform service, but the same God gives ability to all for their particular service. The Spirit's presence is shown in some way in each person for the good of all. The Spirit gives one person a message full of wisdom, while to another person the same Spirit gives a message full of knowledge. One and the same Spirit gives faith to one person, while to another person He gives the power to heal. The Spirit gives one person the power to work miracles; to another, the gift of speaking God's message; and to yet another, the ability to tell the difference between gifts that come from the Spirit and those that do not. To one person He gives the ability to speak in strange tongues, and to another*

He gives the ability to explain what is said. But it is one and the same Spirit who does all this; as He wishes, He gives a different gift to each person.

Because God loves variety, and He wants us all to be special, there is no one single gift given to everyone, and there is no one individual who will receive all the gifts.

So being led by the Spirit, you can shout Jesus is Lord! And you get to live your life in so much joy, love and peace that the smile on your face will brighten up the world around you. The solutions to all of our problems are found in Jesus every day. He is our provider, and our healer. He gives us wisdom for answers to every situation we face as we lean on Him through the Holy Spirit.

He has the right answer to every problem we face. Let Him guide you through the Holy Spirit in you. Ask God for the wisdom of God through Jesus...Ask the Holy Spirit in you to give you a personal revelation of Jesus in the area of your need today.

Grow that personal relationship you have with Jesus by growing the Holy Spirit from within you. The more you connect with Him, the more He connects with you.

Jesus is the solution for every need you have.

Trust Him. Let Him lead you.

Another thing to remember, our spiritual gifts were not given to us for our own benefit. They were given to us for the benefit of others, and other people were given spiritual gifts for our benefit.

God is so good!

The Bible says, a spiritual gift is given to each of us so we can help each other. When we use our gifts together with other believers, everyone around us benefits. If others don't use their gifts, you get cheated, but if you don't use your gifts, they get cheated. This is why God wants us to discover and develop our spiritual gifts.

The Holy Spirit fills us with the traits of Jesus, and He also gives us each special spiritual gifts. All of these things the Holy Spirit gives us is to help us serve the Lord and grow the kingdom of God...helping us spread the Good News.

Ephesians 4:7 (NIV) - *But to each one of us grace has been given as Christ apportioned it.*

Some of those gifts are things like pastoring, prophesying, singing, acting, painting, teaching, building, engineering, and so many more.

What gift has He given you to use for your Christian service?

You might say, Deborah, I've never heard of acting, or building as being a spiritual gift.

When God gives you that special ability that is yours that is in you...and you use it to glorify the Lord, then that is your spiritual ability, your spiritual gift. Not everyone can sing, act, teach, build or whatever that special thing is you can do, but if God has placed a special ability in you, then that is what you are to use to glorify Him...and that makes it the spiritual gift He gave you. Unfortunately not every one uses the gift He gives them to God's glory. That's sad, but true. So as a believer ask Him to help you use the gift He gave you to glorify Him.

The gift He gave me was the gift of gab, and I use it in my writing. Through His grace I am blessed to share Him through my fiction and my non-fiction.

God is so good and loves us so much. We are blessed to be able to share Him with others. And as a believer that is what we are called to do.

Those gifts are given to us by the Spirit for the purpose of sharing Christ with others as the Scriptures above tell us.

Maybe you can think of the spiritual gift given to you by the Holy Spirit as your 'calling'. While you are using the gift the Spirit gives you, this can also put the spotlight on you as a whole.

So be careful and remember your desire should always be letting His light shine through you as you are spotlighting the Lord.

Whereas the Fruit of the Spirit is produced by the Spirit in us and as we develop it, learn about it, and try to walk in it, the more we will become like Christ on the inside, reflecting Him on the outside. I believe the Fruit of the Spirit is His light shining through us.

Praise God!

Ephesians 4:11-12 (GNT) - *It was He who "gave gifts to people"; he appointed some to be apostles, others to be prophets, others to be evangelists, others to be pastors and teachers. He did this to prepare all God's people for the work of Christian service, in order to build up the body of Christ.*

If we want to grow as Christ's followers, we shouldn't focus on how gifted we are or on how well we use our gifts that God has given us. It's what's on the inside of us, our spiritual maturity, that reflects how we are growing as we grow in the fruit of the Spirit.

Walking in the fruit of the Spirit shows how God is transforming our lives as we live more like Jesus every day. With Him we can help build up the body of Christ.

Walking in the fruit of the Spirit involves us dying daily to our flesh and allowing the Holy Spirit living in us to grow bigger and bigger within, helping us to be more and more Christ-like...Praise God!

In First Peter, we are told as a good manager of the gift or gifts God has given us, we are to use it or them, for others' good. And we believers are all to be walking in Christian service in order to build up the body of Christ.

1 Peter 4:10 (GNT) - *Each one, as a good manager of God's different gifts, must use for the good of others the special gift he has received from God.*

In the rest of this book, we will be digging deeper into each aspect of the fruit of the Spirit, helping us to grow and become more and more like Him. Remember as we live our life with God, it does not mean we will be immune from difficulties, but as we stay close to Him and let the Spirit lead, we will live in peace through these difficulties.

Romans 8:6 (GNT) - *To be controlled by human nature results in death; to be controlled by the Spirit results in life and peace.*

The Holy Spirit who lives in us has no experience with being impatient, hateful or rude. That's our flesh acting out when we, the believer, do these things.

When we are living by the Spirit of God, the Holy Spirit will be reflected in us.

I've heard people say things like, "I can't do that. I'm impatient." Or, "I can't help myself." The truth is, as a believer, with the Holy Spirit living in you, YOU CAN! But you have to work on it...dying to the flesh and letting the Holy Spirit in you lead.

And when you fail in living as Jesus would, you are choosing to live by your flesh not His Spirit that is in you.

So change your thoughts and remind yourself you can do all things through Jesus Christ who lives in you. You just have to keep reminding yourself not to do what comes naturally to your flesh, but to try to give the Holy Spirit in you the lead.

Stop and think before you react in the flesh...before you think or say, "I can't help myself. I'm not a happy camper naturally." Or "I can't control myself or my temper."

Remember you don't have to act out in the flesh.

Your Helper is living inside of you waiting for you to defer to Him.

So lean on Him. Let Him lead!

And, don't get me wrong. I'm sure I've said something similar about whatever excuse I was making up for doing things in the flesh instead of letting the Holy Spirit lead me.

The truth is, and we need to realize it, that God gave us the right way to act or react in every situation if we would only take time to rely on Him and let the Holy Spirit speak and act through us.

Take a breath.

Ask the Holy Spirit to lead you.

Learn to take that moment of pause. Learn to let the Holy Spirit lead you, instead of letting your flesh rule. It's your choice. So make the right one, so you can continue to grow and be more like Him as He wants you to be.

Learn to let the fruit of the Spirit shine out in you...through you. Amen!

You can do it. Jesus made sure you could as it says in Romans, 'Clothe yourself with the Lord and stop giving in to your sinful, flesh filled desires.'

Romans 13:14 (GNT) - *But take up the weapons of the Lord Jesus Christ, and stop paying attention to your sinful nature and satisfying its desires.*

Remember what He tells us in Colossians. God loves us and chose us as His own. Take that pause and remember you are His...act like it...or should I say react like it. :)

Colossians 3:12 (GNT) - *You are the people of God; he loved you and chose you for his own. So then, you must clothe yourselves with compassion, kindness, humility, gentleness and patience.*

When we seek God and ask the Holy Spirit to help us grow, we are choosing to deny our flesh and follow the Holy Spirit within us.

Rick Warren reminds us every problem we face is a chance for us to build our character.

And since we want our character to be more Christ-like, we need to remember to lean on the Holy Spirit—not our flesh through every problem and circumstance we face each day. So take a moment when you are tempted to react in a way Jesus wouldn't, and pray for the Holy Spirit in you to lead.

And remember instead of running from our issues or problems, face them.

The Holy Spirit is in you, waiting to take the lead. Let Him. Give it to Him, not your flesh.

Ask the Holy Spirit in you how to conquer that sinful desire and overcome it.

Ask God to do in you or change in you, whatever needs to be changed or done so that the fruit of the Spirit can grow in you and make you more Spirit-minded instead of flesh-minded.

Grow your character today and every day. God gave you the tool to do that very thing...Him...through the Holy Spirit!

It's key to us to look to the Word for the truth about the Holy Spirit. The more you read the Word, the more you will find yourself talking to God. And the more talking to God you are doing, the more you will find yourself praying and praising God.

So talk with God through prayer and praising throughout your day and night. And keep thanking Him for the blessings He keeps pouring out on you. The more you read the Word, the more you will hear the Holy Spirit within you leading you and teaching you Jesus' way.

John 14:15 (NIV) - *"If you love me, keep my commands."*

We need to continue to renew our minds with His Word so our thoughts line up with what God says.

John 16:13 (NIV) - *But when he, the spirit of truth, comes, he will guide you into all the truth. He will not speak on his own; he will speak only what he hears, and he will tell you what is yet to come.*

Again, it is key to us to look to the Word for the truth about the Holy Spirit.

We need to renew our minds with His Word so our thoughts line up with what God says. The Holy Spirit is our power. The Word is our power. Read it and etch it on your heart and in your mind.

Remember, when things get hard that is not the time to quit or give up. It's the time to double up on your reading of the Word; it's the time to double up on your praising God; it's your time to double up on blessing others. It's your time to become immovable and unshakable so Satan can't stop you know.

Jesus has already defeated him and Jesus lives in you, so you are already the victor.

Stand strong with the Holy Spirit in you leading you on keeping your hope in Jesus Christ strong and steadfast.

Romans 5:1-5 (GNT) - *Now that we have been put right with God through faith, we have peace with God through our Lord Jesus Christ. He has brought us by faith into this experience of God's grace, in which we now live. And so we boast of the hope we have of sharing God's glory! We also boast of our troubles, because we know that trouble produces endurance, endurance brings God's approval, and his approval creates hope. This hope does not disappoint us, for God has poured out his love into our hearts by means of the Holy Spirit, who is God's gift to us. For when we were still helpless, Christ died for the wicked at the time that God chose.*

Be patient under trials and keep looking to the Lord for your answers. Then Satan can not get you down! The Holy Spirit is there for you, inside of you, so let Him get you through your problems as He fills you with His hope, victory, and endurance.

1 Corinthians 2:14-15 (NIV) - *The person without the Spirit does not accept the things that come from the Spirit of God but considers them foolishness, and cannot understand them because they are discerned only through the Spirit. The person with the Spirit makes judgments about all things, but such a person is not subject to merely human judgments...*

We need to strive to be more like Jesus every day. We need to let the Holy Spirit in us lead us in His Ways. We need to keep filling our minds with His Word which is the truth.

As we continue to fill our hearts and mind with His Word, His faithfulness will never disappear. He is with us in our best of times and our worst of times.

When you have a problem, go to Him for answers.

He will lead you...if you let Him.

When you depend on Him, His faithfulness in your stormy times, He will be your shelter and see you through it all.

He doesn't keep us from troubles, but He always will see us through them...if you let Him lead you.

Now we will touch on each trait in the fruit of the Spirit so we can grow and become more like Jesus.

God bless you!

LOVE

There are a few types of love. Eros, Philia, Storge and Agape.

Eros is a passionate love, which is what our world most commonly thinks about. It's a love in a romantic sense. It's a physical love. It is love between a man and a woman.

Philia love is brotherly love. It's a love between friends and among equals.

Storge is the natural affection or love, especially of parents for children.

Agape is love of mankind. It's the love God, the Creator of heaven and earth shows us. It's an unselfish love. It is a self-giving love. It's an unconditional love He gives us. We don't deserve it, but He gives it anyway. It is a deeper more truer love than any other love. It is the love we receive from God through Jesus Christ.

His love is perfect and unconditional. And that love again is called agape love, and this is the love we should strive for. It should be our highest goal...to love like God did.

We need to love even when there is nothing in it for us. That is an unselfish love, loving someone because it is what God tells us to do.

We are to love others with no strings attached.

We are to love others to help them, bless them. And doing this, honors God.

God's love is not based on a warm feeling we have within. In fact, agape love is shown in some of the most challenging situations we can find ourselves in.

Jesus showed his greatest love by laying His life down for us on the cross...to save us. He loved us before we loved Him, and He did it unconditionally and sacrificially.

He sacrificed His life to save ours.

When we give the Holy Spirit control in a sticky or confusing situation, then Christ's love can shine through us...if we let the Holy

Spirit take control. The Spirit will help us give up our rights in that situation. He will help us let the other person's rights be more important to us than our own.

That's when we are showing Agape love to another person, and then they can experience the love Jesus gives to us daily.

What a blessing that would be for them...and for us. When we bless others, God blesses us. He is such a loving and giving God.

1 Corinthians 13:4-7 (GNT) - *Love is patient and kind; it is not jealous or conceited or proud; love is not ill-mannered or selfish or irritable; love does not keep a record of wrongs; love is not happy with evil, but is happy with the truth. Love never gives up; and its faith, hope, and patience never fail.*

As a believer, the Word tells us to share God's love. For us to do that we must try to be patient and kind in those demanding situations that come our way. In the flesh, we won't make it every time. But if we let the Holy Spirit in us lead us, instead of our flesh, we can walk in patience and kindness. We must remember not to get jealous of others around us, and for sure not to get proud or conceited when we succeed in something. Remember, we are not alone. We have Christ in us and through the Holy Spirit leading us we will succeed in the things God leads us in and through, by His power. Praise God!

So keep on keeping on, moving forward.

Galatians 5:22-23 (GNT) - *But the Spirit produces love, joy, peace, patience, kindness, goodness, faithfulness, humility, and self-control. There is no law against such things as these.*

Notice when Paul is talking about the fruit of the Spirit in Galatians, love is the trait he mentions first. It is probably because it is the most important trait and because God is love!

The love that is in the fruit of the Spirit is agape love, which is perfect love, good will affection, benevolence (the quality of being well meaning). This love is a selfless love...a Godly love.

1 Corinthians 13:11-13 (GNT) - *When I was a child, my speech, feelings, and thinking were all those of a child; now that I am an adult, I have no more use for childish ways. What we see now is like a dim image in a mirror; then we shall see face-to-face. What I know now is only partial; then it will be complete—as complete as God's knowledge of me. Meanwhile these three remain: faith, hope, and love; and the greatest of these is love.*

The Word tells us as we are growing up learning to talk and to feel and to think, we are growing a faith in our hearts. And in our faith we start to walk in hope.

And as we continue to read the Word building our faith and learning more, we are learning to love as God first loved us. The greatest of these things; faith, hope and love...is love. When we live in love, we live in God, and God is love.

Agape love is the love God feels for us. It is a selfless, sacrificial love. That is how He loves us.

1 John 3:18 (GNT) - *My children, our love should not be just words and talk; it must be true love, which shows itself in action.*

It's a love of choice, not out of attraction or obligation. We are to choose it and then act in it...because God tells us so.

The thing is, to do this, we need to know God loves us, and that is the love we should be showing and giving to others...in our actions. In fact, He told us that in 1 John 3:18. And He told us that He is Love.

1 John 4:7-10 (GNT) - *Dear friends, let us love one another, because love comes from God. Whoever loves is a child of God and knows God. Whoever does not love does not know God, for God is love. And God showed His love for us by sending His only Son into the world, so that we might have life through Him. This is what love is: it is not that we have loved God, but that He loved us and sent His Son to be the means by which our sins are forgiven.*

Jesus Christ displayed His agape love for us on the cross, where He took our place for the sins we committed.

The trait of *love* in the fruit of the Spirit is a selfless, giving love that we receive from God and are to pass on to others.

We should put others' needs above our own. I'm not saying don't take care of yourself. Because when we take care of ourself we are showing God we love Him for creating us to begin with.

Praise God.

He is so good to us.

Love honors others and celebrates truth no matter how difficult it is to hear.

When Jesus was asked which one of God's commandments is the most important, He tells us to love the Lord your God with all your heart and with all your soul and with all your mind. He goes on to say it's the greatest commandment. He continues with a second commandment about love telling us we should love our neighbor as we love ourself.

Matthew 22:37-39 (GNT) - *Jesus answered, "'Love the Lord your God with all your heart, with all your soul, and with all your mind.' This is the greatest and the most important commandment. The second most important commandment is like it: 'Love your neighbor as you love yourself.'"*

Loving God and loving others should always be our response to our Lord and Savior as we live our lives trying to be more like Him.

Agape love in us should encourage us to give of ourselves even when we don't feel like it.

Agape love doesn't let feelings dictate our choices.

When we walk in love we are hopeful. We persevere through everything that comes our way, letting God lead us on what we are to do to walk through any given situation that we are confronted with.

And living in agape love, we are trusting God to lead us as to how He desires us to go. But we have to stay focused on Him and in His Word daily as we live our lives.

So let His Word be our guide on how to let the love of God that was placed inside of us when we were born again, shine on the outside of us letting others see Jesus in us.

2 Corinthians 3:17-18 (GNT) - *Now, "the Lord" in this passage is the Spirit; and where the Spirit of the Lord is present, there is freedom. All of us, then, reflect the glory of the Lord with uncovered faces; and that same glory, coming from the Lord, who is the Spirit, transforms us into His likeness in an ever greater degree of glory.*

So put on the Lord and let the Lord's glory shine through you. His Spirit lives in you. So let His love pour in you and through you to others all around you. As my pastor, Pastor Jonathan Stockstill of Bethany Church in Baton Rouge Louisiana reminded us, love is a filter with which we should do everything.

For sure! Amen!

And always remember love is patient and kind.

While walking in love you won't walk around jealous of what others have. Instead, you are to learn to be content in where you are in your life as you keep connected to the Lord, and also be content with what you have...as long as you are living for the Lord and walking as His Word tells you to walk.

When walking in love you won't go around all puffed up and prideful no matter how bright your light is shining, or should I say, how bright His light is shining through you. It's Him shining through you. Give Him the praise and glory. Thank Him for the hope you have in Him, the trust you have in Him, and the faith you have in Him and for what He is doing through you.

Praise God!

Walk as Jesus did. Let Him lead you in love. Let Him shine through you.

When we live in His love we live in God.

Let His love sweep away any pain that resides in you from what someone else said or did to you. Forgive them and rest in His love for you so you can grow and keep pouring His love out through you to others.

God is so good, and we want to be an example of Him as we walk on this earth.

When loving others we sometimes need to step away from our thinking 'what about me?' and choose to think 'what about them?'

1 John 4:16a (GNT) - *And we ourselves know and believe the love which God has for us.*

Love the people around you so they can experience the love you live in through Jesus Christ. We do this by giving the Holy Spirit control from within us. And then and only then will this fruit of love, this trait in the Holy Spirit in you, come to fruition in you.

John 15:11-13 (GNT) - *"I have told you this so that my joy may be in you and that your joy may be complete. My commandment is this: love one another, just as I love you. The greatest love you can have for your friends is to give your life for them.*

Love is a powerful gift God gives us through His Spirit living in us. If we heed His Word and do what He tells us to do in love, our lives here on this earth are more blessed and free. So love others earnestly.

God even tells us to love our enemies.

Now that's a hard thing to do.

The good news is, He tells us how.

Luke 6:27-28 (GNT) *"But I tell you who hear me: Love your enemies, do good to those who hate you, bless those who curse you, and pray for those who mistreat you.*

He tells us to do good to them. When our enemy hurts us, we are to turn the other cheek and let them hurt us again if they so choose. He also tells us to forgive them.

Whoa, Deborah. There is no way I can do that. Do you know what they did to me? No way. I can't! That would be a very hard thing for me to do.

But guess what. When you don't forgive them, you are only hurting yourself. The one who hurt you has already forgotten about you and how they hurt you and they have moved on to probably doing the same thing to someone else.

So thinking about what they said or did to you over and over in your mind, is only bringing you down.

It's hurting you again and again in your mind and heart as you continue to replay it in your thoughts over and over.

Forgive them so that YOU can move on.

When you forgive them, you will begin to feel the peace of God flowing through you again.

And one more thing He tells us to do, besides forgiving them, we are to pray for them.

You may be thinking right now, that's a bit much, isn't it Deborah?

It may feel like it, but that is what He tells us to do.

Remember, He sees the big picture and He knows what is best for you. And guess what, when we do what God tells us to do we come out so much better. Try it...you will see. God is so good.

Praise God!

Not only has His peace come over us from forgiving them, but as you pray for them to be blessed by God, you will find God blessing you as well. He loves us and loves when we are obedient to His Word.

God is so good to us. His love is so strong. It never fails. And that is what he wants us to live in, His love. Live in it and share it with others.

And remember what Peter told us;

1 Peter 4:7-8 (GNT) - *The end of all things is near. You must be self-controlled and alert, to be able to pray. Above everything, love one another earnestly, because love covers over many sins.*

Walk in the love of Christ, being a blessing and letting His blessings fall on you. Remember His love is unconditional. So let others know the love you are sharing is not conditioned on them believing and acting just as you say or you think they should act. We love others because Christ loved us and died for us. We love others because He told us to.

The love of Christ overcomes all things. And as believers in Jesus Christ as our Lord and Savior, may we all come together in perfect unity, trusting and living the life Christ died for us to live...a life full of love, sharing it with others.

As we believers walk in God's love, this binds us together, showing His perfect love and letting others feel His love which is perfect, making us unified. So as a believer in Christ Jesus as our Savior we are to be more and more like Him. To do this we must walk in His love...which is unconditional and perfect.

Colossians 3:14 (GNT) - *And to all these qualities add love, which binds all things together in perfect unity.*

John 17:22 (GNT) - *I gave them the same glory you gave me, so that they may be one, just as you and I are one:*

1 Corinthians 14:1 (GNT) - *It is love, then, that you should strive for. Set your hearts on spiritual gifts, especially the gift of proclaiming God's message.*

In Romans Paul tells us that the love we show others, should not be fake or pretend. That means the love we are walking in must come from our heart, not just us going through the motions until the unlovable leaves our presence. It is real love, God's love living in us through the Holy Spirit that God placed in us.

So let the love in the Holy Spirit that is within you lead you to express His love to those around you.

Romans 12:9-10 (GNT) - *Love must be completely sincere. Hate what is evil, hold on to what is good. Love one another warmly as Christians, and be eager to show respect for one another.*

Remember, you belong to Christ who loves you. He placed the Holy Spirit in you to help you grow to be more like Christ every day. So let the real love in you shine through to others around you. God's love. As the Holy Spirit grows in your heart, you become more united with Christ and you become more compassionate in your behavior as you walk through your daily lives letting His love flow through you.

2 Thessalonians 3:5 (GNT) - *May the Lord lead you into a greater understanding of God's love and the endurance that is given by Christ.*

Walking in the love of God, letting Him overflow His love in you and through you gives you strength to get through anything and everything that comes your way as you keep growing in the fruit of the Spirit within you.

Ephesians 5:1-2 (GNT) - *Since you are God's dear children, you must try to be like him. Your life must be controlled by love, just as Christ loved us and gave his life for us as a sweet-smelling offering and sacrifice that pleases God.*

The first trait of the fruit of the Spirit mentioned in the Holy Spirit is love. I believe all the traits are important for us to grow, but I also feel to walk in them, we must first grow love. We are God's children and as such we need to be more and more like Him every day.

God is love, and He loved us even though we were not lovable. He loved us before we loved Him. And as His children we are to grow in our love for others...our friends, our neighbors, our families and yes—even our enemies. We are to love all through Jesus Christ our Lord. And we can grow the love in us from God by allowing the Holy Spirit to lead us daily in our life.

God bless you!

JOY

The second trait of the fruit of the Spirit Paul mentions is joy.

So what is joy?

Is joy happiness or the state of being happy? It seems so...but joy and happiness are not the same thing.

Joy comes from God and it is true joy, just like the love He gives us. It is true love.

Happiness, or being happy, is based on a condition or a situation you are in. Someone gives you something you've been wanting and you feel so happy. A feeling of happiness is bubbling up inside of you... a feeling of joy, joy, joy.

But what if it breaks or someone takes it from you? What then?

That happy feeling goes away with it, or it crumbles to pieces...that's joy based on happiness from things; things that come and go as fast as we can blink our eyes.

Joy—true joy—is different. That joy stays with you through any given situation no matter how bad the situation becomes. That's the joy of the Lord living in you through the Holy Spirit. That's the joy within the fruit of the Spirit.

Joy is sometimes felt, but more often joy is a choice. It's a choice you make. It goes beyond a feeling in a positive moment. As believers we are told to choose joy...choose to rejoice in the face of difficulty.

How can you do that, you ask.

You, the believer, can do that because you know who loves you and wants the best for you.

As a believer we choose optimism because we know where we will spend eternity. We look forward to the end of our life here on earth...not that we are anxious to die in our fleshly bodies. Some of us have kids...grandkids...and maybe even great grandkids that we are enjoying seeing them grow. But the reason we can stay joyful, is because we know where our future lies. And we know that when any bad or rough circumstance comes our way, the Lord will see us through.

As a believer, He is our Lord and Savior. — Your Lord and Savior.

So keep your eyes on Him and your trust in Him so you can feel the joy of the Lord grow inside of you...Inner joy that is produced by the Holy Spirit living inside of you. Now that is a glorious thing.

Keep spending time with Him every day in His Word. The more time you spend with Him the stronger you will grow and the easier it will become to overcome every situation that comes your way.

Let the Lord be your strength. Read what Nehemiah says:

Nehemiah 8:10 (GNT) - *"Now go home and have a feast. Share your food and wine with those who don't have enough. Today is holy to our Lord, so don't be sad. The joy that the LORD gives you will make you strong."*

Let the joy of the Lord rise among all you believers. And let the joy of the Lord be your strength. The joy of the Lord is the gladness of your heart that comes from knowing God. The joy He gives us will make us strong.

How do you know Him?

You abide in Him, and He will abide in you.

As you are filled with the Holy Spirit when you put your trust in Jesus as your Savior you know by reading His Word which we know is the truth that He has overcome evil and filled you to the fullest with the Holy Spirit living in you. Now that is cause for joy to overflow in you.

How do you abide in Him?

By reading His Word daily, not just on Sundays with the preacher leading you. Set aside a few minutes or more every day. Make a date with the Word. The YouVersion Bible app offers so many devotionals to read freely every day, and so many versions of the Word to read daily. Grow in the Word and abide more and more in the Lord through reading His Word daily.

And you can grow in His Word by listening to messages of His Word. By talking to Him (praying) often. By singing praises to Him while rejoicing in His goodness. The more you spend time with Him, the more you are abiding in Him. And oh how His joy in you will grow in the Holy Spirit in you.

Praise God for all He does and is doing for you.

When we focus on Him and what He says to us, He helps us through our decision making. He helps us in our action choices and through our behaviors as we communicate with Him daily.

We must always remember as a believer, He is the foundation of our life.

He is our Rock.

He is our strength as we rest in Him. We are to trust in Him to lead us through every situation that comes our way as we walk, following Him in the Joy of the Lord.

Nothing happens without Him. Praise God!

I've heard it said that if the word joy was turned into a verb, the word would be "rejoice." As believers we are told many times to rejoice. So God tells us many times to be in joy.

What a heavenly thought — to be in joy all day long. My heart is doing flip-flops as I think of the joy the Lord is filling me with more and more daily.

Even be in joy in the face of difficulties.

Philippians 4:4-6 (NLT) - *Always be full of joy in the Lord. I say it again—rejoice! Let everyone see that you are considerate in all you do. Remember, the Lord is coming soon. Don't worry about anything; instead, pray about everything. Tell God what you need, and thank Him for all He has done.*

I know that sounds impossible. I can remember having a talk with my sister as she was asking me how anyone could be joyful in the midst of horrible things that are happening in their life at that moment. You can't be joyful...let alone Praise God while it's happening, she had told me.

I prayed a moment for wisdom, before answering her because my sister was a new believer, in her thirties, if I remember correctly, so I wanted to speak where she could understand God's Word and what He is truly telling us in Philippians.

Then it came to me what to say (as His Word tells us He will give us the words He would have us speak. See Mark 13:11).

Finally I answered her. I said, "Don't praise the circumstances you are in. His Word doesn't tell us to do that. Praise the Lord for knowing He is with you and He will see you through these circumstances. That is how you walk in joy in any situation. You praise Him. Keep your trust in Him, knowing He will see you through it.

His Word tells us He will never leave us or forsake us....that is a promise from God.

Philippians 4:4 (GNT) - *May you always be joyful in your union with the Lord. I say it again: rejoice!*

Philippians 4:4 (NLT) - *Always be full of joy in the Lord. I say it again—rejoice!*

So remember to always choose joy. God gives us the wisdom and ability to do so. It doesn't come naturally to us even though we are believers.

We have to make a mental decision to choose joy which is a trait of the Holy Spirit living in us, in you the believer.

And as we choose to live in the joy we are filled with through the Holy Spirit, that trait will grow more and more, developing the "Fruit" within us.

Sometimes joy comes naturally to us as we choose it...other times we have to muster it up in us from deep in our souls.

Joy comes from us knowing who God is rather than who we are or what is going on around us. We have to lean on the power of the Holy

Spirit and find the joy in our difficult situations. We rejoice in Him and keep moving forward as He sees us through.

Today is the day the Lord has made and we are to rejoice and be glad in it. As we do, the joy will fill our hearts.

Psalms 118:24 (NLT) - *This is the day the LORD has made. We will rejoice and be glad in it.*

Find joy, regardless of your circumstances. There are several verses in the Bible that talk about joy to us. Reading them, can help strengthen the joy in you. You can find joy in the Lord through prayer and worship.

Other **Scriptures** to read to encourage joy from within: 1 Peter 1:8, John 15:11, John 16:24, Psalms 20:4-5. And there are many more.

Joy is yours for the taking...yours for the growing. Joy is a fruit of the Spirit already living in you, given to you when you asked Jesus into your heart to be your Savior. Joy is a trait of Jesus Christ Himself. The more you grow the traits of the Holy Spirit in you the more like Jesus you will become.

If you are struggling to find joy today, ask the Holy Spirit to help you. God is a part of you, living in you through the Holy Spirit. He loves you and wants the best for you.

Ask and you shall receive. Ask Him to fill you with His joy and watch Him fill you with supernatural joy.

Allowing God to fill you with His joy at the times you can't bring yourself to do it on your own, will make all the difference in the world. He loves you and He has great plans for you, so trust Him to do what you can't do.

Psalm 71:23 (GNT) - *I will shout for joy as I play for you; with my whole being I will sing because you have saved me.*

If you are blessed with the gift of playing an instrument, use it to play songs of worship to the Lord. If no instrument is handy, then use your vocal chords. They go everywhere you go. Sing a song unto the Lord and watch the joy rise from within you.

As we trusted God for our Salvation, we are to trust Him for each day and his help and strength to get us through the problems that do come with each day. As our roots grow in Him through the Spirit, and we take nourishment from Him, we will grow strong in His Word.

Our lives will overflow with joy and thanksgiving. His joy gives us the strength and confidence to go through everything that comes our way.

Joy will flow out of the wounded places in our hearts and enable us to withstand the most difficult times, because we can rest in Him knowing He will be with us through it all. We need only to keep our eyes on Him and His Word, trusting and believing what He tells us.

Acts 2:28 (GNT) - *You have shown me the paths that lead to life, and your presence will fill me with joy.*

Romans 15:13 (GNT*)*** *- May God, the source of hope, fill you with all joy and peace by means of your faith in him, so that your hope will continue to grow by the power of the Holy Spirit.*

We are called by God to live in joy. So as a believer, no matter what you are going through, you have the joy of the Lord in you to enable you to smile even in the worst of times because God is with you and will get you through it. Hallelujah! Amen!

That's what joy is, happy on the inside because you know God is getting you through this bad circumstance that is happening all around you on the outside. Joy is an internal feeling of great pleasure.

Isaiah 40:28-31 (GNT) - *Don't you know? Haven't you heard? The LORD is the everlasting God; he created all the world. He never grows tired or weary. No one understands His thoughts. He strengthens those who are weak and tired. Even those who are young grow weak; young people can fall exhausted. But those who trust in the LORD for help will find their strength renewed. They will rise on wings like eagles; they will run and not get weary; they will walk and not grow weak.*

Joy is smiling through the bad times because you know the outcome when it passes. It's a special peace we walk in knowing He is in control. Not us. Not others. Our hope is in the Lord.

Romans 12:12 (GNT) - *Let your hope keep you joyful, be patient in your troubles, and pray at all times.*

Remember, our circumstances don't rule us.

We get to choose. So choose joy and walk connected to living in God's presence every day. Thank You Lord!

Psalm 16:11 (GNT) - *You will show me the path that leads to life; your presence fills me with joy and brings me pleasure forever.*

Psalm 51:11-12: (GNT) - *Do not banish me from your presence; do not take your Holy Spirit from me. Give me again the joy that comes from your salvation, and make me willing to obey you.*

When we are walking closely to God, walking in His presence we are filled with His joy.

The Holy Spirit is the source of our joy.

I've always loved the song about joy, joy, joy, joy deep in my heart...down in my heart to stay.

And the good thing I learned as I walked in this joy sharing it with others, it grows more joy in me. Isn't that great?

It's like the more you give away the more that you are filled with. The joy in me is bubbling up inside of me right now just thinking about it.

God is so good!

Joy is rooted in our relationship with the Father, Son, and Holy Spirit.

John 15:11 (GNT) - *"I have told you this so that my joy may be in you and that your joy may be complete.*

God never changes. That alone is a great reason to live in joy, letting the Holy Spirit flow through you as He lives within you. This is a solid base for joy.

My joy, your joy, should be based on who He is, not on how we feel or how our life is going at the time.

True joy is produced by the grace of God. And that joy you are enjoying will get you through the hard times. God is so good. Trust Him. Lean on the Holy Spirit living in you for true joy.

Romans 15:13 (GNT) - *May God, the source of hope, fill you with all joy and peace by means of your faith in him, so that your hope will continue to grow by the power of the Holy Spirit.*

So keep your faith in Him. Keep your eyes on His Word and what He tells you in it. That way when circumstances try to get in the way and take your joy from you, it won't happen.

Why?

Because you are not depending on you.

You are depending on the Lord God Himself. And He loves you and will never give up on you!

Praise God! Thank You Lord!!

PEACE

Another trait of the Spirit is peace. Peace means different things to different people. The dictionary says it's a state of mutual harmony between people or groups. It also states its freedom of the mind from annoyance, distraction, or anxiety.

When you think of peace I imagine, like me, you think of tranquility or serenity.

God offers us peace through a relationship with Him. In fact, He likes to give us a peace that surpasses all understanding.

The good news is we can all walk in that peace if we learn His Word and the good things He tells us in it...and if we learn to keep Him first in *everything* as we walk through life.

I used to read this passage in the Word in Philippians 4:6-7 and wonder what that could possibly mean, a peace beyond human understanding.

Philippians 4:6-7 (GNT) - *Don't worry about anything, but in all your prayers ask God for what you need, always asking him with a thankful heart. And God's peace, which is far beyond human understanding, will keep your hearts and minds safe in union with Christ Jesus.*

I was saved at ten years of age, praise God, and God has stayed close to me and helped me learn more and more about Him and His goodness that He pours out on me and other believers through the years.

By the time I was fifty I had asked myself and God if I would ever feel that peace that surpasses all understanding. Don't get me wrong, God had filled me with peace many many times throughout my life, but over time they slipped from the forefront of my memory. But at different times, He reminds me. Reminding me my peace is in Him.

One major time in my life was at the age of 22 when my oldest child had a brain tumor and the doctors didn't give us much hope...but God did.

He filled me with such peace that I was able to share the peace of knowing God had my daughter in His hands and He would not let this be the end of her life on earth at 3 years old. The peace permeated through me so much it managed to give my husband a peace as well. God walked us through this whole ordeal and before we knew it Rachael was running and playing just like other kids.

I believe that would qualify as a peace beyond human understanding because the world around us had given our daughter a death sentence but the peace of God filled us so full we were able to smile through it all. We knew God had her and would see her and us through the ordeal.

He did this again almost 40 years later when my husband's time on earth was near the end.

Scott and I stayed focused on God's goodness and His plans for Scott that we both felt that special peace that only He can give, the peace that is beyond human understanding because we knew God was surrounding us and getting us through this time, too. Scott and I couldn't explain the peace that we were filled with, but we talked about it, wondering how we could feel so peaceful when death was so near. In our hearts, we knew it was God. Only He can give us this peace that surpasses human understanding.

We knew, it was the love of God that He was pouring out on the two of us. And it was because we kept our trust in Him and His word as we prayed to God asking for His direction in these last days.

We laughed as we realized we were walking in that peace beyond human understanding again...God is so good.

This is what He wants to give us all. So turn to Him always, especially in your times of need, and pray to Him. Stay connected to Him and you too will walk in the peace that is beyond human understanding.

Peter walked in that peace when he heard Jesus say come. Peter knew as a professional fisherman, that he couldn't walk on water. He knew if he stepped out of the boat his whole body would sink beneath the water. His mind knew it, but his heart was being led by the Lord...he focused on what the Lord was telling him to do.

Jesus called Peter and he stepped out in faith and in a peace that was beyond human understanding...and he walked on water. He didn't sink...well he didn't sink right away.

It was only when Peter quit thinking with his heart and started back thinking with his head while looking around at the swelling waters around him, the rough water, and he knew that in the natural he couldn't do this. But another thing happened at that moment as well. He took his eyes off of Jesus and doubt crept in.

So he quit resting on Jesus and started resting on himself. The peace was drowned out with fear of sinking. His peace was gone. Peter took his eyes off of Jesus and lost his peace. And sure enough he started sinking.

Matthew 14:28-31 (GNT) - *Then Peter spoke up. "Lord, if it is really you, order me to come out on the water to you." "Come!" answered Jesus. So Peter got out of the boat and started walking on the water to Jesus. But when he noticed the strong wind, he was afraid and started to sink down in the water. "Save me, Lord!" he cried. At once Jesus reached out and grabbed hold of him and said, "What little faith you have! Why did you doubt?"*

So keep your faith in the Lord strong. Don't give in to doubts. Trust Him to hear and answer your prayers as you keep your heart grateful for God's plans in your life. Trust Him to see you through so you too can have that peace that is beyond human understanding.

Peace is a wonderful and blessed trait to be filled with by the Spirit. Live in it and enjoy the peaceful life God is giving you as a believer in Him.

To keep your heart at peace, you must be forgiving. When you hold un-forgiveness in your heart it permits turmoil in your mind, filling you with resentment which in turn causes unrest in your heart and mind...there goes your peace.

So forgive those who do you wrong, as Christ has forgiven you.

Ephesians 4:32 (GNT) - *Instead, be kind and tender-hearted to one another, and forgive one another, as God has forgiven you through Christ.*

As you continue to feed on the Word and let the Holy Spirit in you grow, the fruit of the Spirit is growing in you as well, and in turn He will help you be a kinder more forgiving person than your flesh would ever lead you to be.

In the natural, which is leaning on our flesh, we are selfish and only think of ourselves as we try to get ahead of where we are in life. Our flesh teaches us to work harder and longer.

I'm saying as you listen to the Holy Spirit within you, you will find yourself using wisdom in the hours you put into your job. Let the Holy Spirit lead you in how you spend the twenty four hour day cycle.

When we say yes to everything that comes our way we can fill up those hours quickly...but is it wise? No. Not always. Learn when to say yes and when to say no.

In fact, in Mathew 36:33 He tells us to put Him first and the other things will follow. So take time to put God first.

But Deborah, I don't have time to read the Word every day.

For your own sake, you need to make time. Maybe turn the television off a little earlier at night, or set your alarm fifteen minutes earlier to start your day. Or on your lunch break find a quiet spot for you and the Lord to spend time together. Those are just quick suggestions.

Look at your life and figure out where you can cut something out or step away for fifteen minutes. In time, you'll find you want to spend more and more private time with Him because He leads you in such peace helping you through your life. And we all know life can be very hard.

John 14:27 (GNT) - *"Peace is what I leave with you; it is my own peace that I give you. I do not give it as the world does. Do not be worried and upset; do not be afraid.*

The book of John tells us Jesus leaves us with peace. In fact, it's His peace that He gives us. He gives it to us as we continue to look to Him for our answers, not the world. This is true peace. Trust Him to lead you on the path He has planned for you, which is filled with His peace that He gives to you. Peace is important if you want to really enjoy your life. He gives us our peace, but we need to hold on to it by not letting ourselves get agitated. Don't lose your temper. It is easier said than done, but it can be done. We have to work on it. Pray for His peace to take over before you let your temper take control.

Jesus is the Prince of Peace. He wants us to live a peaceful life.

Romans 8:6 (GNT) - *To be controlled by human nature results in death; to be controlled by the Spirit results in life and peace.*

Romans is telling us that when we learn to live by the Holy Spirit living in us instead of our flesh that loves to rule us, we will find life and peace. So the more we let the Spirit direct us, the more peace we will find.

So let the Holy Spirit in you grow more every day. Keep renewing your mind with God's Word and let His Spirit control your actions and reactions.

Haggai 2:7-9 (GNT) - *"I will overthrow all the nations, and their treasures will be brought here, and the Temple will be filled with wealth. All the silver and gold of the world is mine. The new Temple will be more splendid than the old one, and there I will give my people prosperity and peace." The LORD Almighty has spoken.*

God is a great God. He loves us so much. He wants to pour out His blessings on us. We are the temple of our Holy God! And our future days will be greater than our todays. His Word tells us so. So as we dwell in His Word, believing God is who He says He is, then we can find and grow the peace of God that rests in the Holy Spirit within us, those of us who believe in Him.

The riches of the world are all His and He wants to give them to us. He wants us to live and walk in a peace that is greater than any peace we've ever experienced before. And He tells us our tomorrows will be greater than our todays.

So keep your eyes looking forward, trusting Him...knowing He's got great plans for you if you only follow His lead.

We are to be armed with the Word of God so we can be ready to share the "Good News" of God's peace. We are to walk in His love pouring it out all around us and His love and His peace will be passed on to those around us as we do.

Live your life living through the guidance of the Holy Spirit within you so you can let God's peace get you through all the troubles and hardships that come your way. The Word tells us plainly that we all will have troubles we will have to walk through, but you must remember you are never alone as long as you are keeping His Word, His love, in your mind and heart. He promises to see you through. Praise God!!!

1 Peter 3:10-11 (NLT) - *For the Scriptures say, "If you want to enjoy life and see many happy days, keep your tongue from speaking evil and your lips from telling lies. Turn away from evil and do good. Search for peace, and work to maintain it.*

Seek peace—Pursue it. Don't just desire peace, go after it.

Have peace with yourself. And have peace with others around you. Read the Word and soak it in. Live as He tells you to.

We are blessed with the Holy Spirit living in us, filling us with love, joy, peace, patience, kindness, goodness, faithfulness, gentleness and self-control so that we can walk and talk as Jesus did, so we can be more like Jesus every day. The most important thing to remember is you have to let the Holy Spirit in you take control. Flesh can't be in control. The Holy Spirit is living in you, the believer, ready and waiting to grow in you.

Spend time daily with the LORD—through His Word, through singing praises—through loving Him and sharing Him with others around you.

When we rest on Him and in Him then we will be in His peace. Listen to His Word and what it tells us to do or not do so we can live in that wonderful peace that He gives to all of His children who follow Him.

Know that He has you. Let Him bless you.

When you start to let worries and troubles get you down, your peace leaves immediately. So don't rest on yourself...rest on and in Him.

Colossians 3:15 (GNT) - *The peace that Christ gives is to guide you in the decisions you make; for it is to this peace that God has called you together in the one body. And be thankful.*

Peace grows in us as we grow in our relationship with Jesus, our Lord and Savior.

In today's world we are bombarded by news media and social media. Most are telling us the terrors of the world. Bad things have happened around the world for centuries, but in today's world we have instant access or instant notifications of those horrors. It's not that things were more peaceful thousands of years ago, it's just the masses of people didn't know about it. When you know about it, you may start to worry about something that may not even affect you or your family, but the knowledge just interrupted that sense of peace you were resting in.

I'm not saying it's bad that the horror around the world is now being told sooner than it may have taken many moons ago, getting the message out...I'm just saying being saturated with the bad news reports puts your focus on those things instead of the future, or your eternity.

If we can and will stay focused on what His Word tells us, we will remember we will get through all the bad that comes our way as long as we keep following Him and His Word and letting His peace keep us calm.

The Word asks us if our worrying about these things will add a single hour to our lives? Guess what? It will not!

Matthew 6:25-30, 33, 34 (GNT) - *"This is why I tell you: do not be worried about the food and drink you need in order to stay alive, or about clothes for your body. After all, isn't life worth more than food? And isn't the body worth more than clothes? Look at the birds: they do not plant seeds, gather a harvest and put it in barns; yet your Father in heaven takes care of them! Aren't you worth much more than birds? Can any of you live a bit longer by worrying about it? "And why worry about clothes? Look how the wild flowers grow: they do not work or make clothes for themselves. But I tell you that not even King Solomon with all his wealth had clothes as beautiful as one of these flowers. It is God who clothes the wild grass—grass that is here today and gone tomorrow, burned up in the oven. Won't He be all the more sure to clothe you? What little faith you have! Instead be concerned above everything else with the Kingdom of God and with what he requires of you, and he will provide you with all the other things. So do not worry about tomorrow; it will have enough worries of its own. There is no need to add to the troubles each day brings.*

So simply put, don't worry about things. Trust God to take care of you and the things you have no power over as you keep sharing Him and growing the Kingdom of God with others. Worrying about what might be won't stop it from happening, nor will it fix it for you. All worrying does is take your peace from you.

Do what you can do and let God do the rest. Trust Him to lead you to do what He would have you do. Quick reminder here - worry about nothing, pray about everything. The world needs our prayers as horrible things keep happening around the world. We need to pray for other believers to stay strong through their tragedy as hopefully others are praying for us to stay strong in those hard times that are hitting us as well.

John 16:31-33 (GNT) - *Jesus answered them, "Do you believe now? The time is coming, and is already here, when all of you will be scattered, each of you to your own home, and I will be left all alone. But I am not really alone, because the Father is with me. I have told you this so that you will have peace by being united to me. The world will make you suffer. But be brave! I have defeated the world!"*

So stay united to Jesus and let His peace cover you. Let Him keep you in peace through any and all suffering that comes your way.

Praise God!

Remember, you are not alone! He is with you and will never leave you.

Wholeness—completeness— tranquility in the soul is true peace.

Allow the Holy Spirit to work in you so He can release a supernatural joy and peace from deep within you.

The Holy Spirit, the fruit of the Holy Spirit, has the power...and releases the power to keep us joyful, calm and stable through everything that comes our way, every circumstance we face—as long as we lean on the Holy Spirit.

John 16:33 (GNT) - *"I have told you this so that you will have peace by being united to me. The world will make you suffer. But be brave! I have defeated the world!"*

So stay in Him and let His peace keep you at rest as you live each of your days to the fullest through the Holy Spirit within you.

A popular verse that speaks of how to live in peace is Matthew 11:28-30.

He tells us to give our worries and our fears to Him.

Try doing that every day. But then leave them with Him. Don't snatch them back.

When you give your worries to Him and take His yoke on you, you will find peace.

His yoke is light and easy. Walk in peace.

Tomorrow is another day — and He will be with you through that one too.

Praise God!!!

PATIENCE

I don't know about you, but from a young age I've always heard patience is a virtue. So what is patience, and what is a virtue?

Off the top of my head, when I think of patience, it's me or you being willing to wait something out without losing our tempers, or like Pastor Mike Haman of Healing Place Church in Baton Rouge Louisiana, said in one of his messages, "Patience is not just waiting, it's how you act while you wait."

He is so right. And as a believer how we act as we wait should reflect Jesus.

Patience is a hard thing to have when bad things start happening around you. One thing we who believe in Jesus Christ as our Lord and Savior must remember is some of those bad things are coming our way because of some choices we made or a choice someone else made that didn't coincide with what God planned for us to choose at that time.

Remember, we all have free will. But the good news is, He will be with us through the happening if we will let Him. Turn to Him and let Him lead you patiently through the situation. And remember, as He gets you through this trying time, even if it is something you brought on yourself. He loves you. Tell Him you are sorry for the wrong choice you made and ask Him to get you back on His path for you.

Because we know His Word tells us He plans good for us, we should know that if we are walking in His plans, good should be coming our way. Of course, sometimes we have to walk through some bad times — trusting Him through it— to come out on the good side that He has planned for us.

That is why the key to patience and peace is to wait on God, trusting Him to lead you and see you through. When we put our trust in Him, and wait on Him, knowing His plans are for the good of us, that is us trusting Him and His Word. So waiting in patience is trusting and hoping in the LORD.

I hope that made sense. I'm trying to say, wait on Him. His time is always the right time.

Pray about your situation. Then turn it over to God. And then be patient...and wait.

When you are praying for God to intervene in your situation, you are usually praying for a miracle...big or small, it is a miracle because you are looking for God's hand to fix things around you.

And while you are waiting on this miracle it is a very crucial time in your faith life. It's the time passing between your prayer and the manifestation of what you are believing God for.

It's the time when things are being set in motion in the spirit realm, and yet in the natural everything still looks the same. It's the time you are most tempted to get discouraged and think nothing is happening and want to give up. But know, as soon as you pray, believing God is listening and knowing He will answer you, (maybe not the way you thought was best) in the best way possible because He sees the big picture and truly knows what is best for you and your situation. This is when you MUST rely on patience. Your patience will keep your faith moving forward, and growing His trait of patience in you. It gives you the ability to wait without wavering—to never give up. Patience is what keeps believing God—even when symptoms persist or bad times keep passing. Patience is one of the keys to receiving that miracle you were praying for. Faith and patience pacs a two punch that puts the devil on the run and brings the impossible to pass! If you've been on the verge of giving up on your miracle, don't. Get back in the ring and this time bring patience with you. Patience is what you need when you are waiting for your miracle.

Patience takes you through the hard places and gets you to victory.

So hang on.

Keep believing.

Keep hoping.

Keep your faith in Him and His Word.

God is so good, but we must keep our trust in Him while we wait in Patience. We are living in a world of instant everything, so we tend to have a hard time waiting...but keep in faith and wait in patience.

The dictionary's definition for patience is the quality that does not surrender to circumstances...or succumb under the trial you are in. If we, believers of Jesus Christ will lean on the Holy Spirit within us, our patience will be strengthened. Patience undergirds all the other fruit of the Spirit listed in Galatians 5:22-23. Patience keeps the other traits of the fruit of the Spirit working in us so that even when we are being weighted down with pressure, we won't give up. Patience keeps us enduring...waiting...persevering.

Stand strong in your faith in God, in His Word, and in His promises. He will never let you go.

Hebrews 6:11-12 (GNT) - *Our great desire is that each of you keep up your eagerness to the end, so that the things you hope for will come true. We do not want you to become lazy, but to be like those who believe and are patient, and so receive what God has promised.*

Hebrews 10:36 (GNT) - *You need to be patient, in order to do the will of God and receive what He promises.*

Now, back to the earlier questions...how is patience a virtue and what is a virtue?

The dictionary tells us virtue is showing high moral standards.

So as believers, it should make us think of how Jesus responded to things around Him. Jesus lived with high moral standards, so as a believer we want to do what Jesus did. We want to take the high road...choose the right responses...the loving responses. We want to be patient in our responses, waiting for the Holy Spirit to lead us in the correct response to the circumstances that come our way.

When we walk in patience, our bodies and minds will stay at a calmness and help us react in a more Christlike way to any given situation.

Proverbs 19:11 (GNT) - *If you are sensible, you will control your temper. When someone wrongs you, it is a great virtue to ignore it.*

The Bible even tells us when we stay calm we are wise...or sensible. So when we wait instead of reacting when someone does us wrong, and we let the Holy Spirit from within respond, we are letting the Lord lead, and that is what we should do.

Wouldn't you love others to see you as a wise person?

Patience is a trait in the fruit of the Spirit from the Holy Spirit, and we are given it as a gift when we accept Jesus as our Savior. The thing is, we need to develop the fruit of the Spirit that is in us—all the traits. That includes patience.

His Word tells us to be patient with others.

1 Thessalonians 5:14 (GNT) - *We urge you, our friends, to warn the idle, encourage the timid, help the weak, be patient with everyone.*

How do you develop your muscles?

You have to work them out. The more you take time every day working a muscle through a sit-up or a crunch, the more that muscle will tighten and become firm. Same with the trait of patience. The more we practice patience, the more patient we will become.

How can we do that?

We have to learn NOT to react instantly.

The key is to wait...pray...listen...then respond. The more we take a moment to pray, listen, then respond, the more patient we will become.

I know it is not easy. Ask any of my family. They have seen and heard me react—instead of waiting patiently— in many circumstances. I'm not proud of it, for sure, but I am thankful that I ask God's forgiveness and He keeps working on me, helping me to be more patient by letting the Holy Spirit in me respond. It takes time...and it takes patience to grow your patience. So persevere. Don't give up.

Fruit isn't instantly ripe.

Have you ever bitten into an apple or a peach before it was ready? I have. It was so disappointing. But when a fruit has matured and ripened, it is so delicious. That bite is so worth waiting for.

We have to grow the traits the Holy Spirit has given us. How do we do that? By reading God's word and soaking it in. The more you grow in His Word, the more ripe your traits will become; like patience will grow in you as you are growing the fruit of the Spirit within you.

Walking in patience as you continue to grow it from within empowers you to keep from damaging your relationships. It keeps you from just saying what pops into your head first. It gives you patience to take the time and think, what would Jesus do?

What would Jesus say?

Develop your patience as you grow in the Word.

Proverbs 14:29 (GNT) - *If you stay calm, you are wise, but if you have a hot temper, you only show how stupid you are.*

Patience through the Holy Spirit is the ability to slow yourself down, to live at a pace of someone else...Jesus. We as believers try to be more like Jesus, walking in His pace, in His peace.

Where there is patience there is peace.

Colossians 3:15 tells us to let the peace that comes from Christ rule in our hearts. Let His Word fill our lives, and be thankful for his goodness and righteousness.

Colossians 3:15-17 (GNT) - *The peace that Christ gives is to guide you in the decisions you make; for it is to this peace that God has called you together in the one body. And be thankful. Christ's message in all its richness must live in your hearts. Teach and instruct one another with all wisdom. Sing psalms, hymns, and sacred songs; sing to God with thanksgiving in your hearts. Everything you do or say, then, should be done in the name of the Lord Jesus, as you give thanks through him to God the Father.*

Love the people around you as you follow the pace Jesus has planned for you, for your life. Don't try to fly through your life. Be in your life moment-by-moment, enjoying what God has planned for you. Walk in peace and patience as you live each day.

Patience is what produces the roots of your faith. Faith gets you going, but patience keeps your faith growing.

Faith does not work quick and fast. Faith believes God will do what He says He will do. And patience keeps you staying strong while waiting to see what you believe for coming to pass ...with your very own eyes.

Patience without faith is a wish. Patience with faith is waiting for God's Word, waiting for God's promises to come through because you know He will. So be patient and wait on God.

That is living by faith. Patience and faith work together, hand-in-hand.

Hebrews 11:1 (GNT) - *To have faith is to be sure of the things we hope for, to be certain of the things we cannot see.*

For us to grow in patience through the Holy Spirit that is in us, we need to continue to live in faith, and be patient. We need to continue to fill ourselves with the Word of God and stand in faith for what God has promised us.

Allow patience to work through you during this time.

Remember you can't have faith without patience or patience without faith. Let the trait of patience in the Holy Spirit work in your life, as you grow the fruit of the Holy Spirit within you.

James 1:2-3 (GNT) - *My, friends, consider yourselves fortunate when all kinds of trials come your way, for you know that when your faith succeeds in facing such trials, the result is the ability to endure.*

Patience is what we need to release through the Holy Spirit in us whenever we are going through any trials that come our way. We know God will see us through as we continue to trust and wait on Him. Let the Holy Spirit's patience see you through.

It isn't easy to go through any difficulty that comes into our lives. We need to always pray about everything, asking God to helps us through, then do all He leads us to do...and then wait...wait patiently for Him to do what you cannot do as He helps you the rest of the way through your difficulty.

God is good. He loves you and wants the best for you. He wants you to walk in love, a very strong and important trait from the Holy Spirit. Patience comes from the love you have for others, God's love.

So keep your faith in Him and wait on Him...patiently and with thanksgiving. Our faith matures as we wait in patience. And His Word and His promises always come through as we keep our faith in Him.

Practice patience by using the Spiritual gift God has given you. As you do, you are helping to grow the Kingdom of God.

This is what we are all called to do...grow the Kingdom of God...by sharing Him and His message with others through your gift, whatever it is — writing, singing, preaching, teaching, caring, healing, comforting others...the special gift God gave you to use to grow the Kingdom of God.

And in serving others, we are to practice patience. If we don't get recognition for what we are doing for others, that is ok. We are not doing it for recognition. We are doing it for God to be known. The more people we bring to know Jesus as their Savior, the more we help grow the Kingdom of God. And that is what He has called us to do.

We want to honor Him as we serve others.

So listen to others around you; hear what they need that you can provide for them through the gifts God has given you. Be a blessing! And be blessed. That is how God works more good into your life as you put others' needs before your own.

1 Peter 5:6 (GNT) - *Humble yourselves, then, under God's mighty hand, so that he will lift you up in his own good time.*

1 Peter 4:10 (GNT) - *Each one, as a good manager of God's different gifts, must use for the good of others the special gift he has received from God.*

So remember as you walk through your daily life with things coming at you from different directions all around you, it isn't easy to stay in peace while practicing patience, but if you keep your faith in Jesus...you will come through the tests and trials that come your way.

Keep waiting patiently on Him and His time, He will bring you through. This too shall pass, but at His timing not yours. Remember He tells us in Psalm 46:10 to be still and wait on Him. Walk in the patience He gave us with and through the Holy Spirit.

After we placed our faith in Jesus by accepting Him as our Savior, He placed the Holy Spirit inside of us. God is inside of you. Trust Him. And wait on Him. Use your patience that the Holy Spirit has supplied for you while waiting on Him.

We are blessed because God doesn't run out of patience on us. We probably push Him to the edge plenty of times. But our God is a good God and He loves us so much, that He continues to show us patience and love even though we don't deserve it.

Thank You Lord.

The important thing for us to remember is to grow in our patience.

How do we do that?

We look at what causes our impatience. It probably starts with fear...fear of losing something or someone. It could be something like your time. If I do this to help them, then I won't have time to do something else I had planned. But you know what? If God put this person in your path who needs your time or your help, He did it for a reason. And you know what Jesus would do? He would help them.

So go for it. Spend the time helping this person. God will bless you for it in so many ways.

Follow Him and His plans for you, doing what He calls you to do. His way is always the best way, as long as you are filling yourself with His Word daily, being fed so you can feed others.

Think about Mary and Martha. Jesus came to their home. Neighbors crowded in, so Martha got busy cooking and preparing to make sure they could feed everyone.

What did Mary do? She sat at Jesus' feet and listened.

When Martha couldn't take it any more, she begged Jesus to get Mary to come help her.

Martha was so busy she couldn't find time to hear the message. But Jesus surprised her by letting her know, she should be listening like Mary was, not cleaning and cooking. That could wait for the time being.

First we should take time to listen to what the Lord has to say and be fed by Him...then we can feed others as He sends them our way.

Luke 10:38-42 (GNT) - *As Jesus and his disciples went on their way, he came to a village where a woman named Martha welcomed him to her home. She had a sister named Mary, who sat down at the feet of the Lord and listened to his teaching. Martha was upset over all the work she had to do, so she came and said, "Lord, don't you care that my sister has left me to do all the work by myself? Tell her to come and help me!" The Lord answered her, "Martha, Martha! You are worried and troubled over so many things, but just one is needed. Mary has chosen the right thing, and it will not be taken away from her."*

Please don't get me wrong. I'm not saying don't help others that come your way. I am saying to make sure you take time to fill yourself to overflow with His Word so you can be the help that person needs.

We are to grow in Him and His Word, and then share Him with others around you. Be prepared. Be patient, and live day to day reflecting Jesus and sharing Him with others.

Be patient and wait on God in your daily life. Live for Him. Follow His lead and He will help you grow your patience.

Praise God!

1Peter 5:6 (GNT) - *Humble yourselves, then, under God's mighty hand, so that he will lift you up in his own good time.*

Isaiah 40:31 (NIV) - *but those who hope in the LORD will renew their strength. They will soar on wings like eagles; they will run and not grow weary, they will walk and not be faint.*

That is the key to walking in patience. You must turn your heart to the LORD.

Trust in Him.

Trust in His Word.

Believe what He tells you above anything anyone else might say.

He is the final Word!

KINDNESS

Kindness, according to the dictionary, is the quality of being friendly, generous, and considerate. Kindness is an action that you choose to make toward others. It is more than just being nice.

In the Word —— the Greek Word - chrēstos - means kind— useful to others.

Jesus tells His disciples to be kind. So He is telling them to be useful to others. And when He is talking to His disciples He is talking to us as well. We believers are His followers so it means we should be like He encouraged His disciples to be...KIND.

Proverbs 11:17 (NLT) - *Your kindness will reward you, but your cruelty will destroy you.*

The Word tells us when we are kind, or walk in kindness, we benefit ourselves.

Several years back, a movie came out called Pay it Forward. After that I heard there where people that did just that. It was always great to hear. I confess, I don't recall ever paying for my meal and then paying for someone else at a table nearby, but the other day my daughter suggested a favorite drive-thru place in the South, Raising Canes, for lunch. They have the best fried chicken fingers and a dip sauce that is out of this world. She said, "How about lunch? My treat!" She is always so sweet, and of course I said, "Sure! Thanks!" We went, and while I was waiting to pull up to the pay window, she said, "Pay for ours and then tell the lady we want to pay for the vehicle behind us as well." I was shocked. I'd heard of people doing that but never experienced it myself. I asked her, "Are you sure?" I know she lives on a fixed budget, but she said, "Yes I'm sure. I do this whenever the Lord leads me, Mom, and have done it for years." I was so proud of her. I did as she said. I know I didn't do it, it was her debit card paying, but it made me feel so joyful seeing the goodness of the Lord pouring out of my daughter.

Thank you Lord for my kids and grandkids. I pray they always see your goodness, and your kindness pouring out of me.

So remember when God leads you, pay it forward. It may be with money, or just a sweet smile or a kind word. God loves for us to share his goodness and kindness everywhere we go.

Luke 6:35-36 (GNT) - *No! Love your enemies and do good to them; lend and expect nothing back. You will then have a great reward, and you will be children of the Most High God. For he is good to the ungrateful and the wicked. Be merciful just as your Father is merciful.*

The Lord tells us to be kind to others...but He also makes it plain that we are to not only be kind to those who are nice to us, but also to those who are not. It's pretty easy to be kind to those who treat you decent, but come on, how can we be kind or good to those who treat us poorly?

That's when we have to rely on the Holy Spirit from within. Our fleshly nature would not repay evil with kindness. But letting the Holy Spirit control your flesh would help you to walk in kindness, even when the other person doesn't deserve it.

So when we walk in kindness, even to those who don't deserve it, even when someone says something to offend us or says bad things about us, what should we do? We know in the flesh we want to lash out at them, tell them they are wrong...or we want to point out their short comings—get their eyes off of us and focus on them.

But no. Don't let your flesh rule. Turn to the Holy Spirit within and ask the Holy Spirit to help you respond with kindness, to respond gently and do it in love.

And we should pray to God to help that person see the error of their ways in how they are putting others down, and maybe even ask God to help them draw close to Him so they won't try to hurt other people with their words any more.

We should also pray blessings upon that person.

Proverbs 15:1 (NLT) - *A gentle answer deflects anger, but harsh words make tempers flare.*

Through Christ all things are possible. But we have to let Christ's Holy Spirit that is living in us who believe in Him as our Savior take control. Let the Holy Spirit lead us into kindness and gentleness, forgiving others just as God has forgiven us.

Ephesians 4:30-31 (GNT) - *And do not make God's Holy Spirit sad; for the Spirit is God's mark of ownership on you, a guarantee that the Day will come when God will set you free. Get rid of all bitterness, passion, and anger. No more shouting or insults, no more hateful feelings of any sort.*

Our flesh wants to repay evil with evil. It's our natural way to react. But we children of God must let the Holy Spirit in us walk through us, and let the trait of kindness permeate our being.

Walking in kindness is a reflection of Jesus in us. When we are walking in kindness through the Holy Spirit that is in us, we are walking in love with our enemies, with those who do us wrong. And when we are doing this, we are pleasing and obeying God's Word.

And then what does He do to or for us when we walk pleasing Him?

He rewards us.

Praise God. He is so good!

Kindness shown to your enemy could start to tear down walls between you and your enemy. Using or walking in kindness helps you win the victory every time.

Ephesians 4:32 (GNT) - *Instead, be kind and tender-hearted to one another, and forgive one another, as God has forgiven you through Christ.*

Extending kindness is a lot harder when faced by someone trying to bring you down. Our flesh wants to react in turn, in defense. But God tells us to be kind to our enemies.

When you respond in kindness it takes the sting out of the one trying to harm you. It may even stop them cold in their tracks.

Respond in kindness and be amazed at how tensions lose their power in the situation. Kindness is not loud, but it's powerful. Walk in it.

Psalm 31:16 (GNT) - *Look on your servant with kindness; save me in your constant love.*

To be kind to one another is an intentional act we as believers should practice doing, but we have to do it on purpose. We have to set our hearts and minds to get up that day to live intentionally kind as we walk through our day in each situation that comes our way. Kindness is a trait that lives in us through the Holy Spirit, but our flesh isn't naturally kind.

So that is why we have to purposely get up and set our hearts and minds into listening to the Holy Spirit within us, not the flesh that just reacts.

The Word goes on to tell us in order to be kind we must forgive.

That, too, is so hard to do. Forgiving others. We've talked about it before. In fact the Word talks about forgiveness a lot, so it is very important. The main thing for us as a believer, we must remember the Word tells us to forgive, so we should.

Most people who offend you, don't even care that they have offended you. Some don't even realize they offended you, so again, why should you forgive them? Because Gods tells us to do so...in His Word, many times. Sure, they don't care. But they hurt you. Do you want to get past or over the hurt?

You can. The Bible tells you how. You need to forgive them. Forgive them, pray for them, then you can let it go and move on.

And also we must remember God forgave us even though we didn't deserve it. When we hold on to un-forgiveness, we are only hurting ourselves. The bad, or sad, thing is if we don't rise above their acts and forgive them, then we are adding on to the pain they just gave us. That only benefits them. It gives them the satisfaction of knowing they did what they set out to do. Hurt you.

Who do you want to be benefitted by your reaction?

God.

Yes.

He is pleased when we do what He tells us to do. And He gives us the power and strength to do it...through the Holy Spirit. Hallelujah!

Psalm 67:1-2 (GNT) - *God, be merciful to us and bless us; look on us with kindness, so that the whole world may know your will; so that all nations may know your salvation.*

Through being merciful and showing your kindness by blessing others, the world around you will know your heart belongs to Jesus and you are saved.

While being merciful, we are to **forgive**. Ask the Holy Spirit to help you forgive them, and then move on.

2 Corinthians 9:9 (GNT) - *As the scripture says, "He gives generously to the needy; his kindness lasts forever."*

Matthew 12:7-8 (GNT) - *The Scripture says, 'It is kindness that I want, not animal sacrifices.' If you really knew what this means, you would not condemn people who are not guilty,; for the Son of Man is Lord of the Sabbath.'*

Kindness is giving hope to those who think they are all alone in this world. We are to clothe ourselves in kindness. You've heard the old saying 'dress for success'? Well God's Word tells us to dress yourself to be kind. You need to get up each morning and pray asking God to help you show His kindness to others around you today. It doesn't come naturally through our flesh, but the Holy Spirit in us wants to show His kindness every day. You must choose to let Him.

Kindness is also seeing the best in others, when they can't see it in themselves. You can give kindness without costing you a penny. Kindness is how you act toward others. It comes from within you.

When we clothe ourselves with kindness we are covered and ready to be the goodness of God in action. We are planning for ourselves to be kind in our actions and reactions. We've planned to keep our flesh quiet, and to listen to the Holy Spirit in us. By letting the fruit of the Spirit flow through us, the Holy Spirit leads us to be more like Jesus every day. But we have to plan to die to our flesh daily and live by the Spirit.

Read the Gospels and see how Jesus acted and reacted in His walk daily. Look to His ministry and how He led people to repentance. Grow in your relationship with the Holy Spirit and His character traits will grow in you, growing the fruit of the Spirit. As we grow in Him we will be drawing more and more people to want to have a personal relationship with Christ as well...again, growing the Kingdom of God. That is what we are all called to do. Share Jesus Christ our Lord and Savior with others.

Kindness becomes who you are when you walk in kindness intentionally, and it is a joyful and peaceful way to live. Let the Holy Spirit shine through you.

Kind people are **gentle and patient** with those who need help. A person showing kindness, walking in kindness, has the ability to be present in any situation and offer the other person a listening ear, a warm smile, or an encouraging word whenever needed. Kindness is to be shared with anyone, and everyone, not just your friends. You can show kindness to strangers on the street. When you do, you are reflecting Jesus, letting the Holy Spirit shine through you. That is the way we believers of Jesus Christ as our Lord and Savior should live, so we can bring more people to the Kingdom of God.

Acts of kindness make the world a happier place to live in.

When you show kindness to a stranger you could be boosting their confidence, and it could encourage them to share kindness with others as well. Again, that's called paying it forward. What a joyful town you would live in if this started happening around you!

The kindest things to do may not be the easiest things to do, but practicing kindness makes us happy.

And allowing unkindness to go uncorrected makes us unhappy.

It's said, that kindness is contagious. So it is definitely something you want to practice, from the inside out. Pour out kindness on others as you walk through your day.

In fact, think about praying each morning before you start your day asking the Holy Spirit to take over in you and pour out the fruit of the Spirit on others. What a great day you would have and what joy you would bring to others.

It is said that kindness stimulates the production of serotonin in the body. And science tells us that serotonin benefits our bodies in many ways; it reduces depression, it regulates anxiety, it calms us down and makes us feel happy. So that sounds like a great reason to walk in kindness. As you are being kind to others you are growing your own self, supplying your body with serotonin making your own self happier.

What a great way to spend your day, being kind to others and lifting your own self up and growing happy feelings inside you.

Kindness is being friendly, generous, and considerate to others and yourself. Being kind often requires courage and strength, as it involves the willingness to celebrate and give attention to someone else. It is also about giving honest feedback when doing so is helpful to the other person. Remember God is with you and will give you all the strength you need. His strength is there for the asking.

Romans 12:15-18 (GNT) - *Be happy with those who are happy, weep with those who weep. Have the same concern for everyone. Do not be proud, but accept humble duties. Do not think of yourselves as wise. If someone has done you wrong, do not repay him with a wrong. Try to do what everyone considers to be good. Do everything possible on your part to live in peace with everybody.*

The word tells us to be happy with those who are happy and weep with those who weep. We are not to think we are smarter than them or better than them. We are to care for everyone and to live in peace with them all. So show kindness to one another and forgive each other as Christ Jesus forgave us.

Therefore, as God's chosen people, holy and dearly loved, we should clothe ourselves with kindness and compassion as we walk through our daily lives.

No act of kindness is ever wasted, no matter how small. Continued kindness accomplishes much. As you scatter and spread kindness around you to other people, it's like planting seeds of kindness that grow and spread.

I was taught as a young girl the golden rule, 'do unto others as you would have them do unto you.' Think about this. If we all showed kindness everywhere we went, the golden rule would mean kindness would be shown back to us. Try it yourself and notice people around you sending kindness back to you. What a beautiful life.

I am from the South and a popular chicken place to buy spicy fried chicken is Popeyes. Their chicken is amazing. The only sad thing was the people who worked at the one near our last home, were never very polite. We would joke about it and say, it's like to get hired at this eatery you have to be rude. If the food wasn't so good, and Scott didn't love the spicy so much, we would have stopped going there for our fried chicken. This is the South. There are other fast food chicken places to choose from. But one day God reminded me of His word:

Matthew 7:12a (GNT) - ***Do for others what you want them to do for you:***

Aha. The Golden rule.

Luke 6:31 (GNT) - ***Do for others just what you want them to do for you.***

In two places in the Word it says exactly the same thing, so for sure God wants us to do this. So the next time the family wanted fried chicken, I went not fretting how I would be treated. Instead, I made a point of being extra kind to the one who took my order and my money.

And I continued to smile no matter what was said to me, and then I made a point of saying something very kind while wishing them a great day or a blessed day, before leaving. And after a month or two of making a point of giving extra kindness in return to rudeness, the workers started being very friendly and nice to me. We all noticed it. So remember to speak in kindness, walk in kindness, showing kindness through you to others, and watch the kindness grow around you.

Practicing the golden rule works wonders.

Remember no matter how unfriendly or rude someone is to you, make it a point to show them kindness. You'll be planting a good seed, a seed that will grow more kindness. It is probably something they need desperately. You never know what they are going through.

And remember, we don't learn kindness by sitting and watching others, we learn by practicing it ourselves...daily.

Kindness is an admirable aspiration for anyone and everyone, and it also can be an effective way to achieve success. By being concerned about others we can build relationships and gain support.

By serving others we can be happier about ourselves.

So pass on kindness, like tossing confetti—throw it everywhere around you. And as you do it to others, I pray, and believe, it will come back to you, just as the Word tells us it will.

Philippians 4:5 (GNT) - *Show a gentle attitude toward everyone. The Lord is coming soon.*

Praise God! The Lord is coming soon. That is the greatest reason in the world to walk around with a smile on your face, showing kindness and being gentle to others. Be happy and share your love of God with others.

Matthew 5:44-46 (GNT) - But now I tell you: love your enemies and pray for those who persecute you, so that you may become the children of your Father in heaven. For he makes his sun to shine on bad and good people alike, and gives rain to those who do good and to those who do evil. Why should God reward you if you love only the people who love you? Even the tax collectors do that! And if you speak only to your friends, have you done anything out of the ordinary? Even the pagans do that! You must be perfect—just as your Father in heaven is perfect.

So walk in kindness and show kindness to everyone around you. Reflect God in you.

GOODNESS

The fruit of kindness and the fruit of goodness are similar. The bible lists them separately throughout the Scriptures, however, goodness and kindness are dependent on one another.

Goodness is the foundation for kindness.

Goodness is the state of being. Walking in goodness is showing kindness to others. When you find yourself thinking more of how you can help others—rather than yourself—that is the fruit or trait of goodness growing in you. When you are more concerned with being a blessing to others than getting blessed yourself; then it is the fruit of the Spirit, goodness, working and growing in you — making you more Christ-like...which is what we as believers should try to be...more Christ-like.

Philippians 2:5-6 (GNT) - *The attitude you should have is the one that Christ Jesus had: He always had the nature of God, but he did not think that by force he should try to remain equal with God.*

The Bible tells us God is good. It's not just something that He has, it is what He is.

It is what He does as well. Good! He is always good, doing good. He never changes. He is good and faithful to us no matter what comes our way.

Life changes.

Circumstances change.

We change.

But God's love and unwavering commitment to us never changes.

In His goodness He always loves us and wants to see us through whatever comes our way.

The Spirit of goodness in you through the Holy Spirit is you doing good for others — putting them before yourself.

Since we were created in His image, it is what we are to be as well. Good. Always loving others, doing good for others, putting them before ourselves.

Through the Holy Spirit within us His goodness is in us — as well as His love, His joy, His peace, His patience, His kindness, His faithfulness, His gentleness, and His self-control.

We were created to do good every day. God has a plan for each of us each day of our lives. We need to let Him lead us to do the good or even the good deed He has planned for us. I believe the more we let the Holy Spirit lead us, the more good we will do daily...like Jesus did.

Acts 10:38 (NLT) - *And you know that God anointed Jesus of Nazareth with the Holy Spirit and with power. Then Jesus went around doing good and healing all who were oppressed by the devil, for God was with him.*

Jesus cared for the poor, fed the needy, healed the sick, and used His resources to meet the basic needs of other people — the ones who came into His life each day. That was Jesus' way, to walk in goodness every day.

So God's goodness is in us, and should be pouring out of us. As it does, we will be producing kindness through walking in goodness. But know we must choose to walk in His goodness.

It is a choice we make. Every day! Wake up each morning and ask the Holy Spirit in you to lead you to do His will for us each day, blessing others as He would have us do. Choose to do His goodness in the world.

We choose right over wrong. If we left it to our flesh to choose, good, unfortunately, is not our flesh's first choice.

Evil comes naturally. So we have to make an intentional choice to let the Holy Spirit lead us to walk in Him, or should I say, let Him walk in us, through us, by the Holy Spirit leading us.

So how do we grow His goodness in us?

We do it by spending more and more time with Him, through His Word, through being in prayer with Him, as well as listening to teachings of Him, and singing and praising Him throughout the day. The more we fill up with Him and His Word and His teachings, the more His goodness pours out of us onto others.

Doing good takes more than good actions. It is His goodness growing in us while we keep connecting to Him. As we do, more of His goodness will flow out of us in our actions, but also through our words. It tells us this in Ephesians 4:29.

Ephesians 4:29 (GNT) - *Do not use harmful words, but only helpful words, the kind that build up and provide what is needed, so that what you say will do good to those who hear you.*

The more you fill yourself with His Word and His goodness, the more you will be like Him as the fruit of the Spirit grows within you.

Goodness is a change that comes into you through the Holy Spirit that is given to you when you become a born again believer.

As the Word tells us when we come to Him, believing and accepting Jesus as our Savior, we will be transformed by the renewing of our mind as we stay in the Word of God.

Take everything that comes against you daily and lay it at the foot of Jesus...at the cross.

He wants to bear your burdens, but you have to give them to Him, and then leave them there, trusting Him to take care of you.

Philippians 4:6-8 (GNT) - *Don't worry about anything, but in all your prayers ask God for what you need, always asking him with a thankful heart. And God's peace, which is far beyond human understanding, will keep your hearts and minds safe in union with Christ Jesus. In conclusion, my friends, fill your minds with those things that are good and that deserve praise: things that are true, noble, right, pure, lovely, and honorable.*

Being confident in the goodness of God changes the way we pray. And as we build our confidence in Him and His Word, our faith grows in His goodness and in His answers to our prayers. So do what the scripture tells you to do, fill yourself with the things that are true. Fill yourself with the things that are right and pure. Don't let the unworthy, ungrateful, terror that roams around the world fill you up. Keep your eyes on Him and His goodness, so you too can reflect His goodness.

Romans 12:2 (GNT) - *Do not conform yourselves to the standards of this world, but let God transform you inwardly by a complete change of your mind. Then you will be able to know the will of God—what is good and is pleasing to him and is perfect.*

God is good. His goodness lives in us, His believers, through the Holy Spirit that is in every Christian, every believer, but we have to let it grow in us. We have to let the Holy Spirit control us...not our flesh.

Psalm 34:4-14, 19-20, 22 (GNT) - *I prayed to the LORD, and he answered me; he freed me from all my fears. The oppressed look to him and are glad; they will never be disappointed. The helpless call to him and he answers; he saves them from all their troubles. His angel guards those who honor the LORD and rescues them from danger. Find out for yourself how good the LORD is. Happy are those who find safety with him. Honor the LORD, all his people; those who obey him have all they need. Even lions go hungry for lack of food, but those who obey the LORD lack nothing good. Come, my young friends, and listen to me, and I will teach you to honor the LORD. Would you like to enjoy life? Do you want long life and happiness? Then keep from speaking evil and from telling lies. Turn away from evil and do good; strive for peace with all your heart. Good people suffer many troubles, but the LORD saves them from them all; the LORD preserves them completely; not one of their bones is broken. The LORD will save his people; those who go to him for protection will be spared.*

David tells us we can see God's goodness in **Psalm 34**. The whole chapter speaks of His goodness and shows us how we should respond to Him. Take time to read it in full.

The chapter tells us how the LORD answered David's prayers. It tells us how He freed him form all his fears. We all have fears that creep in at different times.

Let the LORD free you of your fears. You don't have to hold on to them. You don't have to claim them as your own. Give them to God. He wants to take them from you, free you of them, but you have to give them to Him and let go. Then trust His freedom. David tells us how He saves His people from all their troubles. Again, you just have to turn them over and rest in Him, on Him. David also mentions the angels God sends to guard us, those of us who honor the LORD. And the angels He sends will rescue us from the danger that comes in our lives as we are trusting the LORD to take care of us. We find our safety in Him, with Him, if we so choose to honor the LORD and obey Him.

David goes on to tell us in chapter 34 if we want to live a long and happy life, then we must keep from speaking evil and telling lies. We are to turn away from evil and do good! David tells us that we who are doing good for the LORD may suffer troubles, but He saves us from them all.

We should be thankful for all the goodness He brings our way. We should be happy as we find our safety in Him. Our hearts and words should be thanking and praising Him always.

Praise God, we get to experience His goodness and know it firsthand.

Isn't that awesome?

When we are down for whatever reason, we should share it with God and let Him deal with our issue, or issues. He will. He hears our prayers and answers them. He will never let us stay down as we keep trusting Him and His goodness. The Lord loves us and wants to keep us safe. Honor and believe His Word and He will help you enjoy a long and happy life full of His goodness as you share it and Him with others.

I'm not saying you won't have problems or troubles, but I am saying He will see you through them all as you continue to let the Holy Spirit grow in you and you keep reflecting Him through you. I've lived 70 years, and been saved for 60 of them, so I know firsthand that troubles come, some are even unbearable. But keep leaning on God and His goodness and He will see you through them all. Amen!

God's goodness toward us is given to us—poured out on us freely. We don't deserve it, but He gives it to us anyway. He becomes our shepherd when we give our hearts to Him. He watches over us like a good shepherd...like the good shepherd that He is. We don't deserve it. We don't earn it. He gives us His goodness and blessings because He is Good. We are unworthy, but by God's grace He gives us good things anyway. We are so blessed.

Thank you Jesus!

Titus 3:4-6 (GNT) - *But when the kindness and love of God our Savior was revealed, he saved us. It was not because of any good deeds that we ourselves had done but because of his own mercy that he saved us. God poured out the Holy Spirit abundantly on us through Jesus Christ our Savior.*

God's goodness that we receive is based on His grace and mercy, not on what we've done to earn it. Because we don't deserve it. We are naturally undeserving. But as a child of the Most High God, one of His, He paid the price for all our sins making us pure and clean.

Thank You Jesus!

As we ask Jesus into our lives as our Savior, we are washed in Jesus' blood and made pure in God's sight, and He wants to bless us, pour His goodness out on us. Thank You Jesus. And thank You God.

We are so blessed!

Psalm 118:1 (GNT) - *Give thanks to the LORD, because he is good, and his love is eternal.*

Some people try to tell me God is not as good as I think He is. They ask, if He is so good, why do so many bad things happen?

The truth is, the bad comes from us and others making bad choices, and from Satan who still walks the earth and tries to turn those of us who believe and trust in God, away from Him. But Satan can't take you from your Savior. Satan can, however, stop you/us from being a witness to bringing more lost people to Jesus Christ our Savior.

So don't let Satan rule your flesh. Let the Holy Spirit rule your flesh.

Psalm 145:7-8 (GNT) - *They will tell about all your goodness and sing about your kindness. The LORD is loving and merciful, slow to become angry and full of constant love. He is good to everyone and has compassion on all he made.*

We need to keep declaring His goodness.

We need to let Him shine through us as we walk through our life here on earth.

We need to know that Jesus is always here for us. He helps us grow in our relationship with the Lord as we keep trusting in Him, resting on Him, knowing He has our backs and will not let us down. When we experience difficulties in life we need to keep coming back to what we know to be true.

God loves us. God wants good for us. God is good to us. And He will always work things out for our good...as we keep trusting and resting in Him.

Romans 8:28 (GNT) - *We know that in all things God works for good with those who love him, those whom he has called according to his purpose.*

Through His goodness He has called us...given us a purpose...a purpose to share Him and His goodness with others.

Matthew 5:14-16 (NIV) - *"You are the light of the world. A town built on a hill cannot be hidden. Neither do people light a lamp and put it under a bowl. Instead they put it on its stand, and it gives light to everyone in the house. In the same way, let your light shine before others, that they may see your good deeds and glorify your Father in heaven.*

Let your light shine. Be a beacon of light, reflecting Him.

As His goodness gives us hope, we are to share Him and His love with others giving them goodness and hope. So when we let Him shine through us, we get to pass His goodness on to others...bringing them hope, encouraging them to ask Jesus to be their Savior.

Matthew 5:14-16 (GNT) - *"You are like light for the whole world. A city built on a hill cannot be hid. No one lights a lamp and puts it under a bowl; instead it is put on the lampstand, where it gives light for everyone in the house. In the same way your light must shine before people, so that they will see the good things you do and praise your Father in heaven.*

Keep shining your light...His light in you. The goodness of God leads sinners to repentance. Share Him through your actions in life.

Let His goodness shine through you, through the Holy Spirit living in you, as you bring more people to believe in Jesus Christ, His Son.

2 Corinthians 3:18 (GNT) - *All of us, then, reflect the glory of the Lord with uncovered faces; and that same glory, coming from the Lord, who is the Spirit, transforms us into his likeness in an ever greater degree of glory.*

We need to pray in faith for the sinners to repentance.

We need to show our concern for their well-being.

We need to always reflect the goodness of God as we pray with sincere confidence, believing we are praying to a good Father; a Father who is interested in them, a Father who is caring about all of us. A Father who is on our side...on their side, as they accept Him into their hearts.

Let your face shine reflecting Him!

Psalm 27:13 (GNT) - *I know that I will live to see the LORD'S goodness in this present life.*

God loves us deeply and wants a personal relationship with us, His children.

Praise God!

FAITHFULNESS

God created the heavens and the earth. He is faithful for sharing His glorious beauty on the earth all around the world. Look at all the variety of flowers and trees and their glorious blooms. He created them all.

Great is His faithfulness.

Faithfulness is the seventh trait mentioned to us, given to us through the Holy Spirit living in us. So what does the dictionary say faithfulness means? It says faithfulness is the act of being faithful. So again it is something we are to act out in. We are to strive to be faithful. I said God is faithful. He is faithful to us, the believers of Jesus Christ His son. So who are we to be faithful to? First off and foremost to God. We are to strive to live for Him, being faithful to Him, honoring Him, glorifying Him. We are to strive to live how His Word tells us to live.

He created us. Through His Word He tells us how much He loves us and how much He wants to do for us. His Word is truth. And He is faithful to keep His Word. Praise God!

He is also faithful to continue to do what He says He will do and be who He says He is.

Psalm 119:89-90 (GNT) - *Your word, O LORD, will last forever; it is eternal in heaven. Your faithfulness endures through all the ages; you have set the earth in place, and it remains.*

Thank You Lord, for your faithfulness.

Praise God, He is strong when we are weak. And He never turns His back on us.

He is always faithful. We are the ones who turn our backs on Him. His Word tells us to love our neighbor. We find that hard a lot of times...depending on the neighbor. But He didn't say love your neighbor if he is good to you. We are to love our neighbor no matter how he treats us.

It doesn't mean love what he is doing. Not everyone, including believers in the Lord and in the Word, do what the Word teaches us to do all the time. We want to, and usually try to, but we don't always succeed in living out the Word 24/7.

We are to be faithful to God by loving our neighbor anyway. Love your neighbor despite what he does. That is definitely the time to be praying for God to lead you to share Him with the neighbor. And time to be praying blessings on your neighbor so Jesus can turn your neighbor's heart to the Lord. Maybe your prayers and your actions will help soften his or her heart to hear the message of the Word.

Prayers can open doors.

The good news is, God is faithful to give us that forgiving spirit and that loving spirit so that we can rest on Him, rest in Him, and love that hard-to-love neighbor.

Paul reminds us in 1 Thessalonians that God, who calls us to His Son for salvation is faithful to us. If He gives us a task to complete, He will also give us the strength to complete it.

Thank You LORD!

1 Thessalonians 5:23-24 (GNT) - *May the God who gives us peace make you holy in every way and keep your whole being—spirit, soul, and body—free from every fault at the coming of our Lord Jesus Christ. He who calls you will do it, because he is faithful.*

As God is faithful to us, as being one He created, we should be faithful to Him as well.

How do we do this?

We do it by using the gifts and/or talents He has given us to show others His glory. We are His children and He wants everyone to know about Him, about His faithfulness and love.

But not everyone has been blessed to hear His Word or see His people in action. So as a believer and child of God we are to use our gifts and talents to share God's Word with others. Let us walk in His faithfulness that is in us through the Holy Spirit. Let our faithfulness to the LORD grow so we can bring more people to the Kingdom of God.

1 Corinthians 4:2 (GNT) - *The one thing required of such servants is that they be faithful to their master.*

God is our Master. Let us be faithful to Him. When we are faithful to Him, we have to remember when bad things come our way, we can't give up. God has plans for each of us...and those plans are good. So keep reading His Word. Keep trusting Him. And keep remembering He is faithful to us. Do all of these things as you keep walking through whatever has come your way. The LORD is with you and will see you through.

So let Him lead us to walking the path and doing the plans using our talents, as He has asked us to do, as He is shaping us to be and leading us to do. Thank You LORD!

Our problem is we live in this world of instant. We never want to wait on anything. I say this, because I know that is me and some people I know. We seem to always be in a hurry for everything.

Waiting is the hardest thing I know. But as I keep remembering everything depends on Him, not me, and He is faithful, the good will come my way, and the things He has planned for my life will happen as I continue to wait on Him.

All in His Time. God gave me this as a title for a fiction book He gave me to write several years ago. '*All In God's Time.*' This is so true. We know He will see us through everything that comes our way as long as we keep leaning on Him and trying to walk the path He has planned for us. My fiction books are made up, but my God is real...always...in my fiction and in my non-fiction.

Praise God!

God is so good, and so faithful. So when we practice walking in His peace and love, we too can be faithful and do what He has called us to do as long as we keep walking in the direction He has called us.

His time is always the right time. Don't give up. Keep moving forward. Keep being faithful to Him and His calling for you, despite the challenges you may face. He will see you through. Keep your faith in Him. God will build you up as you walk through your problems trusting Him to see you through. He will mold you and make you the person He has called you to be.

Isaiah 64:8 (GNT) - *But you are our father, LORD. We are like clay, and you are like the potter. You created us, ...*

Isaiah 64:8 (NIV) - *Yet you, LORD, are our Father. We are the clay, you are the potter; we are all the work of your hand.*

So just because trouble comes, don't stop trusting Him. He has plans for you and wants to see you succeed.

Keep your faith in Him as He walks you down and through the path He has planned for you. If we keep listening to Him and letting Him guide us, we will come out stronger than before.

God loves us so much, and when we are doing what He has called us to do, He will see us through. Great is His faithfulness. Let your faithfulness be great as well.

Your faith is assurance in something. As a believer, your faith is your assurance in Jesus Christ, your LORD and Savior. And as a child of God, we have to walk in trust that His Word that we are reading is true. Your faith needs to be strong in the Holy Bible.

It tells us the truth about everything.

He created the earth. He created us. And we can be pure in God's eyes through the blood of His Son—Jesus—our Savior.

As a child of God we have faith in Jesus saving us. We trust He is always there for us because He says so in His Word. We have faith in Him because He is faithful to us. His faithfulness helps us to be faithful to Him.

As we grow in our faithfulness trusting in Him, we grow our assurance on every word He tells us in the Holy Bible. The Holy Spirit in us generates, and grows the fruit in us more and more.

Faithfulness is an important quality in our Christian lives. The more faithful we are to Him, the more fruitful our lives will be as we share Him and His Word with others, bringing them to God...and growing the Kingdom of God.

Luke 16:10a (GNT) - *Whoever is faithful in small matters will be faithful in large ones;*

His Word tells us when we are faithful in the little things, then He knows we will be faithful in the bigger things in our lives. So be faithful to Him and His Word, so He can give you more things to do be faithful in.

God is good. God is loving. We need to always share Him and His ways with others so they will want to be a believer in Him.

2 Thessalonians 3:3 (NIV) - *But the Lord is faithful, and he will strengthen you and protect you from the evil one.*

Faithfulness is unwavering reliability in something or someone. That is what we are to be for the LORD, for He is faithful to us. Through faithfulness we stay constant in our faith in Him who is always loyal to us. Our faithfulness stays strong as we let Him do the work through us.

It's Him—all Him who makes things good for us. With the Holy Spirit living in us, we can endure everything that comes our way. We can persevere through whatever it is, as long as we are leaning on Him, and trusting Him to get us through, letting the Holy Spirit guide us.

Philippians 4:13 (NLT) - *For I can do everything through Christ, who gives me strength.*

God's Lordship is so much greater than any hardships we may be facing or suffering through. We may have to suffer. But through it we will grow. He tells us so...as long as we are leaning on Him. The Lord never changes. He is always there for us to lean on...to lean into. He cares for us and will see us through...any and all things. His strength will get us through. He says so. Trust Him.

Hebrews 10:35-36 (GNT) - *Do not lose your courage, then, because it brings with it a great reward. You need to be patient, in order to do the will of God and receive what he promises.*

This makes me think of what God put in my life...what he led me to do...and how He wants me to share Him with the world. As a young teen I believed God was leading me toward acting—so I could share Him through storylines on stage or in films. But when I was in my early thirties He let me know it was through books; there He lets me perform and share thoughts and actions of all my characters.

He showed me there will be plenty of books written by me, Deborah Lynne, through Him. It started with romance—sweet romance. Then He led me to add mystery in my books. Suspense was added to the mix as well in a couple of the novels. Next He gave me a young adult series to start.

I was loving my writing career and the shape it was taking.

But when my husband passed, my writing came to a stop. I thought it was for good. My grief was so strong, I didn't care if it continued. While I was grieving, I stayed in the Word. I kept resting in His arms for comfort. And I turned to His words daily for encouragement. And after three years, He led me to write my first non-fiction, *'Guidance From The Light.'*

And I stayed faithful in following where He was leading me in my writing.

And I know He will keep leading me as I remain faithful to Him.

So faithfulness is a trait or character of the Holy Spirit that we want to grow in us.

So spread the news, Jesus is LORD. And He loves us and is faithful to us.

Lamentations 3:22-27 (GNT) - *The LORD's unfailing love and mercy still continue, fresh as the morning, as sure as the sunrise. The LORD is all I have, and so in him I put my hope. The LORD is good to everyone who trusts in him, so it is best for us to wait in patience—to* *wait for him to save us—And it is best to learn this patience in our youth.*

Great is His faithfulness, and so should be yours. Let the Holy Spirit grow your faithfulness in Him.

Stand firmly planted, grounded, in your faith in Jesus Christ, your LORD and Savior. Keep your hope and faith in Him. Never stop believing in what He can do in you, through you and for you.

1 Corinthians (NIV) 10:13 - *No temptation has overtaken you except what is common to mankind. And God is faithful; he will not let you be tempted beyond what you can bear. But when you are tempted, he will also provide a way out so that you can endure it.*

Never doubt that the LORD is here for you and everyone in the world who chooses to call on Him to be their Savior. He knows temptations come our way, but remember He is always there to give you the way out. But you have to take it.

It's your choice. So look to Him and follow Him. Take the way He shows you to not give in to temptation.

Receive God's mercy anew every morning and share His love, and joy, and more with everyone you run into each day.

Be faithful to Him and to His Word as He is faithful to you.

God bless you.

GENTLENESS

The definition of gentleness is the quality of being kind, tender, or mild-mannered. Gentleness is being gentle, as Jesus was gentle in His actions and reactions to others around Him.

The Holy Spirit's trait of gentleness in you, leads you to answer people in a gentle way, not accusing, but in a soft loving manner. And this is how we want to respond to others...gently. If you let the gentleness of the Holy Spirit in you grow, you will start acting and reacting in a kind tender manner.

The more you practice responding gently to others, instead of a snapping response in the flesh, the more gentleness will grow in you. Eventually it will become an automatic reaction...because you are letting the Holy Spirit take control.

But when we are letting our flesh lead, we tend to react...not respond. When you respond after taking a moment with the Lord leading your heart, then your response will be in a more gentle manner. So as a believer we should always take a moment to let the Holy Spirit intervene. Let Him lead us in our response in word and/or deed...so you can respond how Jesus would respond.

Matthew 6:14-15 (NIV) - *For if you forgive other people when they sin against you, your heavenly Father will also forgive you. But if you do not forgive others their sins, your Father will not forgive your sins.*

A gentle nature is a forgiving nature.

Jesus forgives us, so we should forgive others. Jesus walks in gentleness toward us, so we should walk in gentleness toward others.

Gentleness in us through the Holy Spirit can be shown in our speech and in our actions.

We as believers don't need to respond instantly to any one or any thing immediately. That is letting your flesh talk for you. We, as believers in Jesus Christ as our Lord and Savior need to learn to take a few seconds to seek the Holy Spirit's way of responding when someone speaks or acts in a "not-nice" way toward you.

We also don't need to be responding in superiority. As a believer and answering in gentleness, we should want to help others, not put them down and build ourselves up.

Philippians 4:5 (GNT) - *Show a gentle attitude toward everyone. The Lord is coming soon.*

Philippians 4:5 (NIV) - *Let your gentleness be evident to all. The Lord is near.*

Let everyone see that you are considerate in all you do.

Remember, the Lord is coming soon. Let your gentleness be evident to all.

The Lord is near. When the Word tells us these things, we as a believer should take heed and act and react in His directions. Others should see us as responding and acting in gentleness… as Jesus did. It's not always easy.

I know. I love my extended family so much and am so glad and proud to be a part of it, but I find lately I've snapped in response to a couple of things said to me. I took it personally. I don't think it was meant that way, but that is how my flesh responded. I was so sorry immediately, and wished I could have taken back my response…but I couldn't. But the thing I could do was immediately ask God to forgive me and soften my heart toward this dear family member. I also prayed for the one who made me feel as their words made me feel. I prayed blessings upon this family member and asked God to help me take that extra second praying and waiting and letting the Holy Spirit respond instead of me. We all have to work on our shortcomings, and have to plan daily to let the Holy Spirit lead instead of our flesh.

Thank You, LORD for never giving up on us. You, LORD, are the best. I praise You for letting me be, letting us be, a part of the family of God.

We as believers want to be more like Jesus every day. And He tells us in His Word, He is gentle.

Matthew 11:29 (NIV) - *Take my yoke upon you and learn from me, for I am gentle and humble in heart, and you will find rest for your souls.*

Our heart, when following the Lord's lead, will find peace and rest. God sees our heart. So for us to be more like Him, we need to be more gentle of heart. We need to humble ourselves.

God loves us and wants the best for us. And that is to be more like Him, so we can be doing what He does for all of us.

What does He do for us?

He pours out His mercy and kindness to us every day. Gently.

He encourages us to do good for others as He does good for us.

Ask the Holy Spirit to help you choose your words carefully. Then to help you speak gently in your response.

Your flesh might want to respond in a way to hurt the one trying to hurt you...but that isn't the way Jesus would respond.

Words are powerful. Like the Bible tells us in Proverbs 18:21, the tongue has the power of life and death. Choose life for you...and for them.

When you return harmful words with kind and gentle words, that usually will take the wind out of the other person's sails and will pretty much stop a fight that the not-so-nice words spoken to you was trying to spark.

Words can hurt—or they can heal.

Let the Holy Spirit in you pour out in gentleness. Stop the fight before it even begins.

Our God is gentle as He pours out His love on us...even though we don't deserve it. He is a merciful God. We are to be like Him more and more every day. Let Him, through the Holy Spirit guide you into walking in love and gentleness. Let Him direct you through His Word and His gentle whispers. Let them guide you to be more like Him in all the situations that come your way.

Pastor Jonathan Stockstill reminded us yesterday in his message that Jesus tells us what to do in both the books of Matthew and of Luke. They tell us we are to — Wait...Go...Make...and Teach.

We are to **wait** on the Holy Spirit. When we wait on the Holy Spirit to lead us on what to say in response—or what to do in response—then we are to, **Go**! Do it! As we move forward, going and doing what the Holy Spirit leads us to say or do, we will be planting good seeds into others, **making** disciples for Jesus. We will be **teaching** and sharing Him with others around us, growing the Kingdom of God.

So wait, go, make, and teach. By growing the Holy Spirit in you and letting yourself reflect Him in your actions and words, more and more people will want what you have. And thank you, Pastor Jonathan for always sharing God's Word and His love to us, the family of God at Bethany.

Let His joy, gentleness, love, and peace flow through you so you can help grow His kingdom.

1 Kings 19:11-12 - (GNT) - *"Go out and stand before me on top of the mountain," the LORD said to him. Then the LORD passed by and sent a furious wind that split the hills and shattered the rocks—but the LORD was not in the wind. The wind stopped blowing, and then there was an earthquake—but the LORD was not in the earthquake. After the earthquake there was a fire—but the LORD was not in the fire. And after the fire there was the soft whisper of a voice.*

The Lord talked to Elijah in a whisper...a soft voice. And sometimes He talks to us in the same way, through the Holy Spirit living inside of you the believer.

Psalm 119:105 - (GNT) - *Your word is a lamp to guide me and a light for my path.*

Let His light shine, leading you on the path He has planned for you.

In the scriptures above He directs us with a quiet voice whispered in you and sometimes to you through others. Be alert and available to share God's love and Word with others...while using the gift of the Holy Spirit He gave to you. Let His gentleness be revealed through you.

Walking in gentleness does not mean you are weak. When you are being gentle in your walk, it's you submitting to God's will. It is you knowing He will get you through. It is you doing the good things God has planned for you. Walking gently shows, not you, but the Holy Spirit is in control.

Psalms 37:7-9 (NIV) - *Be still before the LORD and wait patiently for him; do not fret when people succeed in their ways, when they carry out their wicked schemes. Refrain from anger and turn from wrath; do not fret—it leads only to evil. For those who are evil will be destroyed, but those who hope in the LORD will inherit the land.*

When you do, not only is your speech the evidence of God's gentleness in you, but your actions can be—will be—too when you wait and let the Holy Spirit lead you. Walk in the Spirit—NOT in the flesh when someone speaks poorly or not nice to you, or about you. Respond in His gentleness with the help of the Holy Spirit.

We were made in God's image. God reassures us when we get down and turn to Him to help us through, He lifts us up. His Word encourages us to be who He made us to be—a reflection of Him so we can do our part in growing the Kingdom of God.

He uses His gentleness to encourage us. He pours out His kindness in gentle whispers. When we sin—which we all do—but as believers we don't want to—He is there for us, never leaving us or forsaking us. When we sin we know as a believer we are going against God and His plans for us. We can't be happy when we are sinning because we are going against God's Word. His Word is our road map to living the life He called us to live...in His image.

Romans 8:9 (GNT) - *But you do not live as your human nature tells you to; instead, you live as the Spirit tells you to—if, in fact, God's Spirit lives in you. Whoever does not have the Spirit of Christ does not belong to him.*

Romans 8:11 (GNT) - *If the Spirit of God, who raised Jesus from death, lives in you, then he who raised Christ from death will also give life to your mortal bodies by the presence of his Spirit in you.*

Live by the Spirit—not your flesh.

When walking in gentleness, your response to fellow believers or fellow family and friends is not to judge them when you think they have done or are doing something wrong. Instead, pray for them and their situation. And if God leads you to, you can share your thoughts or worry gently and in love with them. But the main thing for you to do, is go to God in prayer for them, letting Him work with them and their situation. Let Him do the correcting and directing. Speak only if He tells you to, and do it through the Holy Spirit...in love.

Exodus 14:14 (GNT) - *The LORD will fight for you, and all you have to do is keep still.*

Exodus 14:14 (NLT) - *The LORD himself will fight for you. Just stay calm."*

The Lord will fight for you and them. Moses tells us so. All you, the believer have to do is keep still...stay calm and wait on the Lord...while praying for others!

When you are walking in gentleness and making way for God to handle things, you will reap the benefits of gentleness.

The Bible tells us things will go right for you. Things will work for you and you won't lack anything.—When you are letting Him lead you through your life. And then your life will be more peaceful and blessed.

Thank You Lord.

Walk in the joy of the Lord every day by letting the Holy Spirit lead you.

Matthew 5:5 (GNT) - *"Happy are those who are humble; they will receive what God has promised!*

Matthew 5:5 (NLT) - *God blesses those who are humble, for they will inherit the whole earth.*

His Word tells you, those who walk in gentleness, will receive the promises God has given His believers in His Word. That's all of the promises He has meant for His children, not just one or two. God loves us and loves to bless us with His promises. Read the Word and know what belongs to you, His children. We will inherit the whole earth. Praise God!

Psalm 37:11 (GNT) - *but the humble will possess the land and enjoy prosperity and peace.*

He goes on to tell us we will enjoy prosperity and peace. Hallelujah!!!

So how do we grow the attribute of gentleness from the Holy Spirit that is inside of us?

By spending time in the Word. We cultivate the traits, God's traits, that are found in the Holy Spirit, by spending time in the Word. By spending time in prayer. By spending time in worship.

So we know, we grow gentleness from the Holy Spirit by spending time with Jesus. Amen!

Be humble and gentle as the Word says. And do it through the love in you.

Ephesians 4:2 (NLT) - *Always be humble and gentle. Be patient with each other, making allowances for each other's faults because of your love.*

Put others before yourself. Help them, and Christ will take care of you. Pray for those who do evil...do not join in their ways. Lift them up to the Lord in prayer and stay in the Spirit, letting Him guide you, being humble...being gentle.

Philippians 3:2a (GNT) - *Watch out for those who do evil things,*

In living your daily life, you are to watch out for those who do evil. Don't join them in their plight. Walk in the Holy Spirit, reflecting all the traits of God that live in you. It's not always easy to walk in gentleness, but when you let the Holy Spirit continue to grow in you, that trait of gentleness will be more and more prevalent in your life.

The Word tells us when someone offends you, hurts you, or makes you angry, the flesh wants to strike back immediately—but if we can take a moment to pray and give it to God—then wait on the Holy Spirit to guide you, with your response, you will be able to move forward in His peace.

So the key is waiting on God to lead.

And sometimes He tells you not to say anything. That works as well. It may be hard sometimes...but we can do that if He tells us to. We just have to listen and respond to Him. Never respond in the flesh. Respond in the Spirit. Remember, silence is sometimes the answer. For me that's hard. I don't know about you. But over the years I am learning more and more on how to be patient and wait on the Holy Spirit to lead me.

Galatians 6:1 (GNT) - *My friends, if someone is caught in any kind of wrongdoing, those of you who are spiritual should set him right; but you must do it in a gentle way. And keep an eye on yourselves, so that you will not be tempted, too.*

Like Galatians 6:1 tells us - if someone is doing wrong, going against God's Word, you are to tell them—but tell them in gentleness if the Holy Spirit so leads you to say anything. Again, Sometimes He tells us to stay silent. So listen.

And be sure to watch yourself so you are not tempted to join in.

1 Peter 3:15 (NIV) - *But in your hearts revere Christ as Lord. Always be prepared to give an answer to everyone who asks you to give the reason for the hope that you have. But do this with gentleness and respect, ...*

As believers we should always remember to revere Christ. He is our Lord and Savior. This should show in our actions and reactions toward others.

And when people see you not respond in the flesh as they may think you should do, but instead they see you take a moment...a pause...you wait a moment or two, because you've asked the Lord for guidance. Now you are waiting on the Holy Spirit in you to lead...then you act...as the Lord led you to act.

Gentleness is displayed in the way you act and react toward one another. Your actions and speech reveal the gentleness in you when you let the Holy Spirit lead you.

When we give a gentle answer, it may make the one who was not doing or saying right, think twice about what they had just done. And they see you didn't react in the flesh (as others will see as well), so then it might make them change in their actions...and it might have someone asking you why you were kind when someone deserved a comeuppance...at least that is how the flesh sees it when someone verbally or emotional attacks you.

This gives you an opportunity for you to share the love of Jesus with others. Awesome!

Proverbs 15:1 (GNT) - *A gentle answer quiets anger, but a harsh one stirs it up.*

So always take a moment to share that your hope is in the Lord. And your hope is in eternity in the Kingdom of God. Praise God. What a glorious way to live your life...and grow the Holy Spirit in you.

Titus 3:1-2 (GNT) - *Remind your people to submit to rulers and authorities, to obey them, and to be ready to do good in every way. Tell them them not to speak evil of anyone, but to be peaceful and friendly, and always to show a gentle attitude toward everyone.*

In today's world with things going as bad as they are, it is easy for us to point the finger at some of our leaders in our government. Yes, they could be making wrong decisions for our country, or state, or city, but in the end, remember it is Satan using them to try and hurt those of us who believe in the Lord.

So remember our leaders are in charge over our country because the Word says so. It tells us that He placed them in authority over us. And if we are blessed to live in a country where the people vote the leaders in, then we put them in office. Our job now, is to pray for them to grow in their leadership, and pray they listen to the Lord to guide them as well.

Don't speak evil over them. Instead, pray for them to connect with the Lord and let Him lead them.

Exercising gentleness in situations produces peace. It shows you relying on God for His vengeance, not yours. He says in Romans 12:19 - vengeance is the Lord's.

Romans 12:19 (NLT) - *Dear friends, never take revenge. Leave that to the righteous anger of God For the Scriptures say, "I will take revenge; I will pay them back," says the LORD.*

When you let the Holy Spirit lead you, trusting Him and His strength, then you are reacting in power. His power. We know He knows what is best for us—always.

And remember, gentleness is not weakness. It is controlled strength. And when we rely on the Holy Spirit for our gentleness, that strength is God's...the greatest strength of all.

SELF-CONTROL

The dictionary's definition of self-control is the ability to control oneself, in particular, one's emotions and desires or the expression of them in one's behavior, especially in difficult situations.

A great scripture for believers to stand on is 2 Timothy 1:7.

2 Timothy 1:7 (GNT) - *For the Spirit that God has given us does not make us timid; instead, his Spirit fills us with power, love, and self-control.*

POWER, LOVE, AND SELF-CONTROL.

Wow!

Take that in.

As a believer we are filled with the Holy Spirit the second we ask Jesus to be our Lord and Savior, inviting Him to fill us with His Spirit. And this scripture tells us the spirit does not make us timid and shy...instead His Spirit fills us with a power more than we had on our own. It's power from the Lord.

And His Spirit fills us with a love like His.

This love, when we let the Holy Spirit be in control, loves without expecting something back. We give it freely because that is how Jesus pours His love on us. Freely.

A gift not deserved, but given to us anyway. And the last but not least of what Timothy tells us the Holy Spirit in us does for us, is it teaches us self-control.

Self-control helps us to be more like Jesus.

The power, love, and self-control from the Holy Spirit helps us to represent Jesus. And that is how He has called us to reflect Him in our actions, in our words, and in our speech. So as a believer we should rest more and more on letting the Holy Spirit in us lead us.

Let the Holy Spirit have control...not our flesh...not our first thought.

We have the Holy Spirit in us, rely on Him.

Let Him lead you in your response. This is how we will be more like Jesus, when we let the Holy Spirit lead us in response to any and all situations that come our way.

Titus 2:11-13 (GNT) - *For God has revealed his grace for the salvation of all people. That grace instructs us to give up ungodly living and worldly passions, and to live self-controlled, upright, and godly lives in this world, as we wait for the blessed Day we hope for, when the glory of our great God and Savior Jesus Christ will appear.*

Stay rooted in God's grace. His grace tells us to give up our worldly fleshly desires. As a believer we should desire what the Holy Spirit in us desires.

The Holy Spirit in us desires good things to happen to others around us. We should want to do good for others. We should be happy when others are blessed.

God blesses us and it makes Him happy to see us walking in His blessings. And when others see you being blessed, they want it too. So as God is blessing you, show your joy in the smile on your face. Show your happiness in Him even as bad things are happening around you, for you know His Word tells you that whatever bad is happening around you at the moment, God will see you through, directing you in the direction you should go. And as you are going through this difficult time in your life but letting God lead you through, He will also be helping you grow through it as well...grow as a Christian, grow as a believer.

Proverbs 3:5-6 (NLT) - *Trust in the Lord with all your heart; do not depend on your own understanding. Seek his will in all you do, and he will show you which path to take.*

The key to self-control is seeking His will, doing what He would have you do...not following or doing what your flesh leads you to do. Ask Him how He wants you to be or handle this situation, then follow His lead. Not your own way, but His way. The more you let Him lead you, the more you will have self-control interacting as Jesus did, not as your flesh would have you react.

James 1:2-3 (NIV) - *Consider it pure joy, my brothers and sisters, whenever you face trials of many kinds, because you know that the testing of your faith produces perseverance.*

Keep your eyes on Eternity, and what He has for you. Persevere through the trial. And you will grow in self-control.

Use self-control in reaction to the things happening to you and around you. Use self-control around the people around you doing or saying whatever they say or do...even when it's against you. Let the Holy Spirit be your guide every time. The more you give up control to Him inside you, the more your flesh will learn to be more like Jesus. Praise God. Again, persevere.

Galatians 5:16 (GNT) - *What I say is this: let the Spirit direct your lives, and you will not satisfy the desires of the human nature.*

As a believer in Jesus Christ as your Lord and Savior, you don't want to let your flesh control your day. You want to let the Holy Spirit inside of you lead you.

Let yourself turn control over to the Holy Spirit living in you. It's hard to do, because we automatically want to react...which is us acting out in the flesh, our flesh. But when you take a second...a moment...to raise up a quick prayer - 'help me Lord', 'lead me Lord'... the Holy Spirit will direct you. But you have to have enough forethought in you to know to pray.

God hears us—and He answers us.

The more we take those seconds here and there asking the Holy Spirit to lead us, the more we grow in self-control. The more you turn control over to the Holy Spirit in you, the more natural it will become for you to react through the Spirit instead of reacting in the flesh. And in turn you are growing your self-control, giving it to the Holy Spirit within you.

Praise God!

John 14:15-17 (NIV) - *"If you love me, keep my commands. And I will ask the Father, and he will give you another advocate to help you and be with you forever—the Spirit of truth. The world cannot accept him, because it neither sees him nor knows him. But you know him, for he lives with you and will be in you.*

This is a promise you can trust and rest in and be assured of forever. When you ask Jesus into your heart, the Holy Spirit comes in to stay and reside in you. And the great thing is, when you grow in the Word and let the Holy Spirit grow in you, you will find yourself making better choices. You feel more at peace with the world and your life around you.

And I believe life becomes easier because you are letting the Holy Spirit lead you.

The Holy Spirit is the spirit of God, so when you are listening to it, you are listening to God direct you. Stay attuned to the Holy Spirit in you and you will find your life here on earth more joyful, more peaceful, more productive.

The ease of life will be yours.

Don't get me wrong. I'm not saying that everything in your life will be perfect. Nor am I saying it will be easier. I am saying when trouble comes, you will know how to handle it and get through it. And you will come out even better after you've walked through your problem with the Holy Spirit guiding you. And that's when the ease of life will be yours. That's because you are resting in the Lord and knowing He is in control, not you.

Remember, if we don't have self-control, we will be slaves to what ever controls us — more food, more money, more words, more drink—having more, more, and more things. When we let other things control us then we will find ourselves living in the consequences of not having self-control. And not living in the ease of life.

Living in self-control is the start and foundation of living a life of righteousness, which is what we strive for as a believer in Jesus Christ. To be and live more like Him.

And remember, even though you are striving to live in self-control, you are not going through life alone. Well, you don't have to do it alone. You just have to remember to ask Him for help, and He will always give it to you...because He is always there with you, never leaving you or forsaking you.

Last night I had a perfect example of that. If you know me, you know I've had a weight issue all my life. Is it because I was made that way, and there isn't anything I can do about it?

Absolutely not.

My problem has always been I don't use self-control when it comes to eating. I'm not a lover of food, I am a lover of snacks. Snacks are not usually healthy...even when you try to use celery or raisins or grapes, or things of that nature for a snack. At least in my case, I should say. If you are like me, you add peanut butter, or squeeze cheese or cream cheese to give the healthy snack more flavor. Haha. Defeating the reason for eating the healthier snack. I love eating peanut butter with almost anything, and I don't mean a teaspoon. Or cheese, if you want me to eat a vegetable, then cover it in cheese and man I will eat it up. Ha-ha.

You have to use self-control when you eat, what you eat, and how much you eat.

Same is true for other things that control you instead of you controlling it.

Anyway, last night about 10:30 PM I thought, man, I'm hungry. I want something. But truly, I wasn't hungry. I mean it's practically bed time. I probably had just seen a commercial for a food I like, but my mind told me I wanted something. I thought for a moment before I got up and followed my flesh, God, if I give in to this desire, I will never lose that excess fat. Help me. Stop me.

As soon as I offered up this short but to the point prayer, I heard in my Spirit say ... You don't need anything. You're going to bed shortly and you are satisfied. I've got you.

I promise you, that desire left me when I listened after I spoke with Him.

Sometimes we ask, but we don't wait or listen for a response.

He is always with us, but we have to do our part, speak with Him and listen for His response, and then follow.

I was up maybe thirty more minutes tops, and then went to bed. This morning I weighed (as I do every morning) and had finally dropped another pound.

Slow but sure. Had I not taken a moment to ask for help, I know I would have given in to the flesh and had that unneeded snack. And I would have gone 2-4 tenths of a pound up, instead of down. Now I need to persevere in turning to the Holy Spirit in me for help instead of giving into my flesh.

This is the same with anything that controls you other than the Spirit.

Get help from Him, letting Him help you have self-control more and more in whatever tries to keep you as a slave to it.

If you struggle with self-control, know the Word of God can and will help you grow in your heart and mind.

His Word has the power to remind you of His truth and will help you make the right decisions in your life if you let it...if you let Him.

Always remember one step-at-a-time, and one day-at-a-time. But keep moving forward, and looking forward. Don't look back.

Look into His word and keep moving forward.

1 Corinthians 10:13 (NIV) - *No temptation has overtaken you except what is common to mankind. And God is faithful; he will not let you be tempted beyond what you can bear. But when you are tempted, he will also provide a way out so that you can endure it.*

This is a great scripture to remember. Read it and keep it in your heart and mind.

That way, when you are tempted to let your flesh indulge in what you know is not right, or not right for you, take a moment to remind the Lord of His promise to you (just as Jesus did when He was being tempted by Satan),

"Please Lord, you said you would not let me be tempted beyond what I can bear. Right now my flesh is very weak. Take this temptation away from me...or squash its nagging at me. Give me your strength to turn away. Grow my strength to bear more so I don't give in...or help me walk away. Thank You Jesus."

Proverbs 16:32 (GNT) - *It is better to be patient than powerful. It is better to win control over yourself than over whole cities.*

As scripture tells us, self-control is an important trait to have.

In fact, it is a powerful trait to have and use.

So look within yourself to the Holy Spirit living in you, and let that trait grow.

Praise God!!!

CONCLUSION

Romans 12:1-2 (GNT) - *So then, my friends, because of God's great mercy to us I appeal to you: Offer yourselves as a living sacrifice to God, dedicated to his service and pleasing to him. This is the true worship that you should offer. Do not conform yourselves to the standards of this world, but let God transform you inwardly by a complete change of your mind. Then you will be able to know the will of God— what is good and is pleasing to him and is perfect.*

Strengthen the traits of the fruit of the Spirit in you and watch the light from within you grow brighter and brighter. That is the LORD shining in you. So let His light shine bright. Renew your mind and stand apart from the world and be Holy.

Fruit comes from roots growing deep in the ground, getting stronger as they are fed and nourished. So grow stronger by nourishing yourself with the Word of God. Let His roots grow in you — love, joy, peace, patience, kindness, goodness, faithfulness, gentleness, and self-control.

Remember always, God is with you and will never leave you. You might turn your back on Him, but HE WILL NOT LEAVE YOU. Deuteronomy 31:6.

Deuteronomy 31:6 (GNT) - *Be determined and confident. Do not be afraid of them. Your God, the LORD himself, will be with you. He will not fail you or abandon you."*

Keep your faith and trust in Him with any situation that comes your way and **know that He will see you through.**

Let Him always be your source of strength, your source of peace, your source of love.

God is love and He loves you and wants to help you through whatever comes your way, but you must believe His Word is truth. And as you continue to put your hope in Him, He will continue to grow your roots of the fruit of the Spirit in you.

We humans are the only ones made in God's image. We are spiritual beings. We think, reason, and solve problems. We can give and receive love to our fellow humans. We have a conscience. We can discern right from wrong. We are accountable to God.

Sin is what damaged us and still damages us when we choose to walk in sin.

So God sent Jesus to restore the full image of God in us, the image we lose when we walk in sin. So through Christ, us covered in His blood, God sees us more and more like "the image of God," — how He intended in the beginning.

How do we know what Jesus' image represents and shows?

The Word tells how.

Stay in it.

Renew your mind daily with the Word.

Jesus walks in peace, love, joy, and so much more. This is the fruit of the Spirit. So as we are saved through accepting Jesus as our Savior, He fills us with the Holy Spirit, receiving the fruit of the Spirit. And to grow in the Spirit we must learn what each trait is by walking in the Spirit - letting Him lead, not by walking in our flesh, like Satan wants us to do.

2 Corinthians 4:4-5 (GNT) - *They do not believe, because their minds have been kept in the dark by the evil god of this world. He keeps them from seeing the light shining on them, the light that comes from the Good News about the glory of Christ, who is the exact likeness of God. For it is not ourselves that we preach; we preach Jesus Christ as Lord and ourselves as your servants for Jesus' sake.*

Satan, however, as you just read, wants to blind people from the Word of God, keeping them lost.

We believers want to reflect Jesus. And we want to be all He's called us to be.

Most of all we want others to see Jesus in us. We can accomplish this by being more like His image, which again is being loving, joyful, peaceful, patient, kind, faithful, gentle, good, and in control of oneself.

We who believe in Jesus Christ as our Lord and Savior do know that Jesus Christ is the Son of God. Jesus Christ is God who came in the flesh to save us.

God's word confirms this.

Colossians 1:15 (GNT) - *Christ is the visible likeness of the invisible God. He is the first-born Son, superior to all created things.*

Christ is the visible image of the invisible God. It goes on to tell us that through Him God created everything in the heavenly realms and on the earth. He made things we can see from things we can't see (from nothing). Everything was created through Him, by Him, and for Him.

He existed before anything else. God holds it all together for us. Christ is the head of the church. And the church is the body of Christ...we who believe that Jesus Christ is our LORD and Savior.

When we gave our hearts to Jesus Christ our Lord and Savior we were included, adopted into the body of Christ and to the family of God.

As a result we are holy and blameless as we stand before God without a single fault. But we must continue to believe this truth and stand firmly in it.

Don't drift away in your belief. Stay strong and deep in His Word.

Stay standing, believing, remembering and acting in your faith.

Praise God for loving you.

Praise God for sending His Son to save you.

And praise God for the opportunity He gives you to reflect Him by growing the fruit of the Spirit within you, making you more and more like Jesus Christ your Lord and Savior.

The day you decide to walk in the Spirit and not in the flesh is the day you decide to be all God called you to be. It's the day you let the Spirit direct you throughout your life.

The moment you step across the line and put your faith in Christ, God forgives you and gives you grace and eternal life.

Romans 5:15-16 (GNT) - *But the two are not the same, because God's free gift is not like Adam's sin. It is true that many people died because of the sin of that one man. But God's grace is much greater, and so is his free gift to so many people through the grace of the one man, Jesus Christ. And there is a difference between God's gift and the sin of one man. After the one sin, came the judgment of "Guilty"; but after so many sins, comes the undeserved gift of "Not guilty!"*

The first thing Jesus did was wipe the slate clean for you. He wiped out everything you've ever done wrong. It's forgiven!

There is no condemnation.

Such grace!

With the grace you receive eternal life. It's God's long-range plans for us.

The Bible tells us in Romans 6:23, that the wages of sin is death, but the gift of God is eternal life. You can never work your way or earn your way into Heaven. The only way you'll ever get into Heaven is by God's free gift that you accept by faith.

So let God live through your life as you let the fruit of the Spirit grow within you and pour out on others.

When you embody the fruit of the Spirit: love, joy, peace, patience, kindness, goodness, faithfulness, gentleness, and self-control, you become more like Jesus and you bring more people to salvation, growing the Kingdom of God.

The fruit of the Holy Spirit is the effect of living the Christian life in obedience. It flows through those of us who have accepted Jesus as our Savior as we are letting the Spirit lead us instead of letting our flesh control us. We are walking in obedience to His Word resisting the "works of the flesh," as it speaks of in Galatians.

Galatians 5:18-19 (GNT) - *If the Spirit leads you, then you are not subject to the Law. What human nature does is quite plain. It shows itself in immoral, filthy, and indecent actions;....*

The flesh produces WORK but the Spirit produces FRUIT. Fruit is a good and wonderful thing we produce when we let the Holy Spirit live in and control our lives.

Galatians 5:22-23 (GNT) - *But the Spirit produces love, joy, peace, patience, kindness, goodness, faithfulness, humility, and self-control. There is no law against such things as these.*

So as a believer, filled with the Holy Spirit, let the Holy Spirit lead you in the choices you make.

Try not to give into your flesh. — listen to the Holy Spirit instead.

By listening and giving into the Holy Spirit not your flesh, the Holy Spirit within you will grow more and more in you every day. Hallelujah!

God bless you as you stay connected to Him.

Praise God!

A prayer for you to pray daily

Dear Heavenly Father
Help me walk in the fruit of the Spirit...all
nine traits.
Grow You within in me, Jesus,
and let me reflect You in all I do.
In Jesus name I pray.
Thank You Lord! Praise You!
Amen!

Acknowledgments

I want to thank God first and foremost for trusting me with a message He wants me to share with my readers. I was blessed at an early age of ten to find Jesus as my Savior and invite Him to live in my heart. Throughout my life He has helped me through many challenges and led me through the difficulties that came my way. I am seventy years of age now and have been through many difficult situations in my life, but God is always true and faithful in being with me and helping me through these times in my life.

Last year He put this idea for a new book, another non-fiction that He wanted me to write—growing the Holy Spirit from within. I know when I heard this from Him and I had no idea where to begin, let alone know what to say, but I did know He would show me when the time is right. So I started reading some of my favorite peoples work who spoke on the Holy Spirit, people like Kenneth and Gloria Copeland; Beth Moore; Pastor Joel Osteen; Pastor Joseph Prince; and more, so many more. I also used the YouVersion Bible to read many 'plans' on the Holy Spirit, which of course led me to a lot of Scripture to help me grow in my understanding. After many months of reading and researching the Word and other people's teaching, the Lord led me to begin.

My book is not long...it's an easy read...and I am thankful for the direction God gave me in sharing the Holy Spirit with you the believer, and helping you to see He has plans for you and through you reading His Word you will grow the Holy Spirit in you and in turn help Him grow the Kingdom of God as you let the Holy Spirit shine through you.

Thank you for taking time to read my book, and may God continue to bless you in His Word and in His plans for you. I am also blessed to be part of the family of God and get to grow in my wisdom and understanding through Pastor Jonathan Stockstill and the family of Bethany World Prayer Center. If you haven't found the church that helps you grow, pray for God to lead you to a church near you where the pastor shares the Word and God's love with you always.

Take care and God bless you always.

Deborah Lynne

MY PRAYER

Dear Heavenly Father.

Thank You for the Words You have given me to share with others in this latest book, **Growing the Fruit of The Spirit**.

Bless each and every reader as they read the book You gave me.

Grow the fruit of the Spirit within them as they lean on You, trusting You in their life. Grow the Holy Spirit in them with Your wonderful traits and lead them to follow Your plans for them.

Help me to keep seeking your direction for my life and in my writing. I know I'm not doing it on my own ability. I'm doing it by Your ability. I'm not looking at what I can do; I'm looking at what you can do through me. I'm letting the size of You, my God, determine the size of my dream.

Help me to keep moving forward, as you grow my dream. And help me to keep remembering that all things are possible with you. Keep me strong in You and in Your Word, resting and trusting in You to guide me through Your plans for me.

In Jesus' name I pray,

Amen.

Other Books by Deborah Lynne

Non-fiction:
Guidance from The Light
Blessings from God
But God Says...
Growing the Fruit of The Spirit
Samantha Cain Mysteries:
Be Not Afraid
Testimony of Innocence
The Truth Revealed
Against Her Will
Stand-alone mystery/suspense:
Crime in The Big Easy
Hidden Secrets
Passion from the Heart
Coming in 2025, untitled Crime in The Big Easy book 2
Coming in 2025, untitled Passion From the Heart book 2
Romance:
Second Chances
All in God's Time
Grace, a Gift of Love
Young Adult Fiction:
Chasing The Lights book 1 Cooper Parks Adventures
Coming in 2024, Listen Closely (book 2 of the Cooper Parks Adventures)

Bayou Secrets - a compilation of 3 of Lynne's mystery novels

About the Author

Deborah Lynne, mother of three, grandmother of five, is blessed to share her love for God through her writings in her fiction as well as her non-fiction. When Lynne started writing at 33 years of age, she thought God had called her only to write fiction and share His love for us through it.

A few years ago He encouraged her to write her first non-fiction, ***Guidance from The Light***, a one-year devotional.

This book is filled with Scripture God shared with her through a sad period in her life...the loss of her husband after 43 years of marriage. For over two years she stayed deep in the Word. Then during her third year of loss, God led her to write the book, ***Guidance from The Light***, released in 2017. Two years later, she was led to write a second non-fiction, ***Blessings from God***. This book, too, is based on what God's Word Says. Again, its contents were encouraged by God. He loves us and wants to bless us...and wants us to know this. It was released in June 2019. ***But God Says***. Was the next non-ficition God led her to write and was released in 2021. The latest non-fiction is **Growing The Fruit of The Spirit.**

In 2022 Deborah started back on one of the three fiction book ideas God had given her to write. Again, God intervened and had her put them on the back burner again as He led her to write about the fruit of the Spirit. The others are important to Him, but this is what He plans for her to release now—All in God's Time and all in His direction, she says.

Ms Lynne hopes you enjoyed - ***Growing The Fruit of The Spirit***. She assures you more books will be released in 2024. And she is thankful that you continue to stay in touch while keeping up with reading her writings.

Deborah is a mother, a grandmother, an ex-secretary, retired dispatcher, and widow who God has chosen to share His love and His presence, with others, and she is proud to do it. So as she alters 'a little' what she used to say to everyone who would listen, she now Says — **Some** of my books are fiction, some non-fiction, but God is real in every one of them.

Ms. Lynne hopes you enjoyed reading her book, hopes you dug deep into the Word as you read her latest novel ***Growing the Fruit of The Spirit...*** She loves sharing Him with you.

At present, her fiction is available in eBook form for $3.99 for each download from most eBook reader sites. Her **non-fiction** in eBook form is **free** on most eBook reader sites. All of her novels, fiction and non-fiction are available in book form at various prices through various venues such as Kindle, Barns and Noble, walmart.com[1] and more. See her website for more information. Lynne's Website - **author-deborahlynne.com**[2]

Three books have been released in audio form. The latest was ***Crime in The Big Easy***. More will follow.

1.	http://walmart.com

2.	**http://author-deborahlynne.com**

www.ingramcontent.com/pod-product-compliance
Lightning Source LLC
Chambersburg PA
CBHW031433150726
47989CB00002B/929